lifelong relationships and str[...] ing up in Brooklyn in the '40s [...] thirty years of experience in a variety of legal roles, I still rely on humane lessons learned while sitting on the edge of my seat in Dr. O'Kane's classroom at Drew University. They remind me that defendants, police, and probation officers are also individuals entitled to the respect and decency that all of us deserve as participants in the New Jersey Criminal Justice System."

— Andrew M. Baron, Esq.
Managing Partner
Kochanski, Baron & Galfy

"These pages open a window to a time before New York City's current renaissance — a time when people defined themselves primarily by their ethnicity and misunderstanding fueled distrust, stereotyping, and even violence. Most Brooklyn residents of today would not recognize this portrait of their beloved borough sixty years ago and might even be appalled. But James O'Kane experienced it firsthand and recounts what it was like to grow up in that world. He weaves some charming stories of youth to which we can all relate while preserving the uniqueness of coming of age in a city where diverse ethnic groups were still growing accustomed to living in close quarters."

— Mark Young
New York City Resident
and Brooklyn native

Jefferson Avenue

Stories from a Brooklyn Boyhood
1941-1958

James M. O'Kane

JEFFERSON AVENUE
Stories from a Brooklyn Boyhood 1941-1958

Copyright © 2013 James M. O'Kane

ISBN-10: 1493767046
ISBN-13: 978-1493767045

Published by James M. O'Kane, www.Jim-OKane.com

Cover and book design by Bill Ash, Cape House Book Services
www.CapeHouseBooks.com

Cover photograph: Brooklyn Museum/Brooklyn Public Library, Brooklyn Collection

Some names and identifying details have been changed to protect the privacy of individuals.

Publisher's Cataloging Information

O'Kane, James M.
Jefferson Avenue: Stories from a Brooklyn Boyhood 1941-1958/by James M. O'Kane.

     p. cm.

ISBN-10: 1493767046
ISBN-13: 978-1493767045

1 2 3 4 5 6 7 8 9 10

For my grandchildren

Mary Alina
Caitlin Rose
Christine Marie
James Patrick
Michael Joseph
Tiernan Xavier
Andrew Joseph
Colleen Grace
Joseph Davin
Thomas James
Declan Michael
Joseph Ryan
Hannah Kyrie
Noreen Rose
Paxton Hugh

Contents

Tilly/Mammy

Let me start this book by telling you about my mom and her life and background. My sisters Helen and Bernadette and I often remark what a truly crucial role our mom played in our upbringing and emotional development. We often remind ourselves that Mammy, or Tilly (Matilda) as her friends called her, could have chosen a different path after our father died in February, 1944. Some advised her to remarry and start a new life, while others advised her to place us in an orphanage and think about herself. Still others advised her to return with us to Ireland and pursue a rural life on the farm of her in-laws. Ignoring all of this well-meaning take-care-of-number-one advice,

Mammy thought little about herself and did what she believed was best for her three children. She later told my sisters and me that it was the hardest decision of her life. Within a four-year period, she had married, bore the three of us, and lost a husband through death. By any standard, a bleak future awaited her. However, for our sake, she placed us in the forefront, and in our opinion, did an amazing job raising us — often to the surprising dismay of others who could not imagine a widow doing so. Thinking of herself first wasn't Tilly's way.

The O'Kane family traces its origins back to Northern Ireland, to County Derry, to the area between the towns of Dungiven and Garvagh, to a glen known as Glenulen, or, as our family simply called it, The Glen.

My knowledge (which I learned in stories and histories handed down in the family) extends only so far back as the life of my maternal grandmother, Tilda (also Matilda) who was born in 1872 in Limavady, County Derry. Orphaned at age six, she was raised by two uncles who treated her as a mere servant, and raised her to support them economically. By the time she reached adolescence, some of her older sisters, who had emigrated to America, sent money for her passage there. But the uncles concealed and squandered the money, unbeknownst to Tilda. Only after angry letters from America did the uncles relent and allow her to leave Ireland. Her ordeal almost sounds like a chapter of a Dickens novel!

In 1888 Tilda emigrated to Philadelphia where she obtained employment as a servant in a doctor's home at a salary of $3 per week, plus room and board. She met and wed my grandfather Michael Mullin (circa 1892), another immigrant. Everyone called him "Big Mickey" since he stood six feet six inches tall. They eventually came to Brooklyn, New York, where Big Mickey worked as a paver on the

Collection of James M. O'Kane

Tilda and Big Mickey.

recently constructed Brooklyn Bridge, which earned him a salary of $50 per week, an enormous amount in 1900. Before he married he would sail to Ireland every fall, money in hand, and live "like a king." He returned in the spring when work on the bridge resumed. Mickey made that crossing seventeen times. Tilda made the crossing six times. They eventually settled permanently in the Glen where they purchased a farm and raised three children: Willy, Patrick, and Tilly, who was born in 1911. There were two other siblings who died at birth.

Big Mickey must have been considered a formidable character. Tall and strong, he loved to look for fights in New York City and often on weekends engaged in the drinking and brawling so characteristic of the immigrant Irish. This peculiarly Irish tradition consisted of Irish saloon patrons engaging in a virtual donnybrook brawl on Saturday evenings. But this brawling could have dire consequences. One weekend, Big Mickey and his brother Huey ventured into a tough area (possibly in Harlem) looking for a fight. On this occasion, they encountered five toughs and proceeded to fight them until one of the toughs pulled out a knife, an action beyond the rules of Irish brawling. Big Mickey almost killed his assailant in the ensuing struggle. The knife-wielder ended up in a coma and police arrested Big Mickey and charged him with aggravated assault. My grandmother Tilda purchased a bottle of whiskey, brought it to the local police precinct, and presented it to the Irish desk sergeant. This resulted in Big Mickey's speedy release. I guess you might say that the Irish took care of each other. Fortunately, the knife-wielding victim survived and was released from the hospital a week later. Big Mickey died in Ireland in 1917, probably from complications from diabetes, and my grandmother tried to manage the farm. But economic and political times were tough in the ensuing years.

In those times Ireland tore herself apart in the era of the Black and Tan conflict (named for the color of the uniforms of the British squads sent to Ireland in 1920-1921 to quell the Irish insurrection against English rule) and the subsequent Irish Civil War, 1922-1923.

Our family sided with the factions opposed to British rule. My mother's brothers Willy and Pat served as a teenage "runners," shuttling messages in the hills around The Glen to IRA fighters. The eventual peace accord dictated that Ulster and Derry separate from the Irish Free State since those in Ulster favoring union with England (Protestants) outnumbered those seeking union with Ireland (Catholics) two-to-one.

My mom, born in 1911, too young for active participation in these "Troubles," often spoke of how everyone in the family was terrified of the Black and Tans who regularly menaced their area, hauling her mother and two brothers out of their home for midnight harassment and random searches. Simultaneously, the family encountered the animosity of the Protestant Unionist majority of Derry who favored continuing political ties to England. This often resulted in overt hostility that regularly manifested itself on July 12, the celebration of the Protestant victory under William of Orange ("King Billy") over Catholics at the Battle of the Boyne in 1690. My mother would recount how Protestant and Catholics got along reasonably well until Orangemen's Day when the local Protestants would jeer, harass, mock, and spit at the Catholics. But on July 13 everything returned to normal with reasonably civil relations between the Protestant merchants in Garvagh and their Catholic customers.

By the mid-1920s, Tilly's brothers Willy Mullin and Patrick Mullin left Ireland for America. Unable to run the farm alone without male support, Tilda and Tilly sold it and came to Brooklyn in 1931 aboard the steamship Transylvania. Tilly was nineteen and found work as a nanny, taking care of various children in New York City, including George Plimpton, a literary celebrity years later.

Tilly's older brother Willy never really adjusted to America and moved to London in the late 1920s and lived there until 1952 when he again came to Brooklyn. While in London, he drove one of the city's legendary double-decker buses. Fond of alcohol, he drank every chance he got. On one occasion during the Blitz (the German bombing of London in the fall of 1940), he returned to his rooming house, blind drunk, and fell asleep in his room. When he awoke the next morning, the external walls of the entire building had been demolished by Nazi bombs, leaving Willy and his cat alive. Miraculously he survived unscathed while everyone else in the rooming house had perished. His second attempt at American life lasted only a few years. Dissatisfied again with life in the USA, he returned to London, married at age sixty-eight, and eventually died in 1967.

Tilly's older brother Patrick found work in a milk plant, Sheffield Farms in Brooklyn. His marriage to Betty Mullin in 1940 eventually failed, and when he visited us on Jefferson Avenue he treated my sisters and me as if he were our actual father. Mammy continually bemoaned the fact that he lived alone in a rooming house without a proper diet or someone to care for him. In 1950, he died suddenly after cutting himself shaving, contracting erysipelas (a serious skin disease), which resulted in septic shock.

Let me now briefly tell you about my grandfather's family. My grandparents Ellen and James O'Kane also resided in County Derry's Glen, in the Brockaghboy section. Married in 1904, they raised ten children with my father Bernard O'Kane, born in 1905, the oldest. Five immigrated to the United

States, one to Scotland. My father came to Brooklyn in 1927, joining his brother Frank.

My father and Uncle Frank lived in a rooming house in the Williamsburg section of Brooklyn, then, as now, a largely Hasidic Jewish neighborhood. Each became what the Hasids termed a "Shabbat Goy," that is, a Gentile who could do manual tasks (e.g. lighting kitchen stoves, extinguishing candles, switching on electric lights) on the Sabbath day since Hasidic Jews are forbidden to work on Shabbat.

In that rooming house, everything was not as it appeared. Next to their rooms lived a middle-aged woman with a cat that liked to walk along the fire escape ledge, enter my dad's kitchen, and eat the food on the table. Nothing seemed to dissuade the furry thief from doing so. Finally in desperation, my dad and Frank lured the cat into the kitchen, put it in the oven, turned on the gas, and waited. They eventually removed the terrified beast just short of its suffocation! For some reason the cat never came back, and its owner registered total dismay when she noticed that her cat would cringe in terror when it encountered the Irish terrorists. "I don't know what's wrong with Tabby. She seems so afraid of the two of you." They never let on about their aversion technique of dissuading Tabby's unwelcome intrusions.

From the start, my father had serious medical issues. Suffering from tuberculosis in Ireland, he had a number of relapses and numerous hospitalizations here in America, undoubtedly aggravated by his heavy cigarette smoking (three packs of Raleighs a day) and by his occupation as a subway conductor on airless New York City trains. He and my mother had known each other in Ireland, dated in Brooklyn, and married in 1940. Tilly was always aware of his precarious health, but his death was still a shock to her. Together with Tilda, they lived for a year on Quincy Street, a few streets away from Jefferson Avenue.

Collection of James M. O'Kane

My parents' wedding (1940). L-R: Eddy Donaghy, Aunt Betty and Uncle Pat Mullin, Uncle Frank O'Kane, Grandma Tilda, Tilly and my father, Aunt Lena and Uncle Ray Delvalle, Uncle John and Aunt Mary Barton.

Sadly, my father died at age thirty-eight in February, 1944. I have only two distinct memories of him. I remember the first one clearly. He and Uncle Frank took me for a walk on Ralph Avenue and bought me candy. I believe that I was a little over age two at the time. The second memory relates to his dying from complications of pneumonia. Father Devanney, a priest at Our Lady of Good Counsel, came to our apartment to administer my father the Last Rites. I can clearly recall the darkened room with the two lighted candles and a crucifix near his bed. I turned three four months later. I have no memory of his funeral, but my father's sister Aunt Helena often tells me that the hearse and dozens of cars and hundreds of mourners passed by our Jefferson Avenue apartment in homage following his funeral Mass.

I often wonder how Tilly ever dealt with such a trauma. At the time of my father's death, she was five months pregnant with Bernadette (or Bunny, as we nicknamed her). Left virtually indigent, she had no real income, but our relatives, always generous, helped us monetarily whenever they could. I recall a few years later many of my relatives giving me "a wee penny," in reality a few dollars, to help us. Never would they give the wee penny directly to Mammy since this would have been demeaning. Things deteriorated so rapidly economically that our family went on welfare ("relief" in those days). Mammy hated this since the welfare investigator would appear unannounced at our apartment, open the refrigerator and ask why there was anything beyond mere subsistence in it. The welfare people would also question why three children needed new shoes or an extra dress. We seemed to be regarded as crooks, stealing from the public treasury, squandering the public dole.

Fed up with such humiliating treatment, Mammy tried to find work. Thank God our Granny Tilda lived with us and minded us, for without her we probably would have been sent to foster care or even an orphanage. Mammy worked at various jobs: serving as a ticket agent on the New York subways; cleaning homes for doctors on Bushwick Avenue; running an elevator at the Angel Guardian Home (where my godmother's sister was a nun); working as an attendant at St. Catherine's Hospital (where my sisters and I were born); cleaning offices at the Cotton Exchange on Wall Street; cooking dinners for the Franciscan Brothers at Our Lady of Good Counsel. Often these jobs overlapped and Tilly usually worked twelve to thirteen hours each day, six days each week. She told me that she would work all day, come home, make dinner for us, and then go out to her night job cleaning offices. Many times she would get home at midnight, fall into bed, rise at 6 a.m. and start the routine all over again. Granny took care of us, making all this possible. Somehow, Mammy and Granny got through this terrible time. Years later, Mammy told me, "For seven years after your father's death I didn't know if I was coming or going! It was my Catholic faith that kept me afloat."

Family members and so many friends helped where they could. My grandmother's cousin, Uncle Eddy Donaghy, opened a savings account in a Manhattan bank—far from the snooping welfare investigators—to help us financially. My uncles and their buddies would appear unannounced with cans of paint to decorate our apartment, saying, "Tilly, take the kids for ice cream and get out of here for a few hours." Christmas toys would arrive from Santa (actually the good nuns from the Angel Guardian Home), though one year they arrived December 26 since Santa's reindeer "got lost!" Helen, Bunny, and I were heartbroken that Christmas but overjoyed when the presents finally appeared. Santa hadn't really forgotten us! Neighbors on Jefferson Avenue, particularly Nan Fee, Mrs. Behan, the McCabes, and Johnny McClorey's, Peter Fiorillo's and Tommy Luhmann's moms—all helped out in whatever way they could. The priests, brothers, and nuns of Our Lady of Good Counsel also took our family under their wings. Certainly for me, the brothers and priests became surrogate fathers, guiding me through the treacherous currents of childhood and adolescence.

Foremost among these helpers were Father Francis McCabe and Father Matt Kelly. Father McCabe often brought Holy Communion to my ailing grandmother. When we were run out of our Jefferson Avenue apartment by its mean-spirited new landlords, Father McCabe helped us secure a much better apartment on Halsey Street. But Father Kelly went even further. When he learned that Mammy and four other office cleaners at the Cotton Exchange had been fired (and replaced with recent "displaced persons" from Poland at much lower wages), he referred her to a close friend of his, the Director of Personnel at the N.Y. Telephone Company who hired Mammy to clean offices each night at a generous salary. She got great benefits, and, best of all, free phone service! We had struck it rich!

Mammy did well at the phone company. After four years of cleaning offices, she received a promotion to the position of elevator operator, with regular daytime hours, and a handsome uniform to boot. She loved this new role. After the elevators became fully automated a few years later, she stayed on as an elevator dispatcher, a job she kept till her retirement in 1977. Over those years Mammy had acquired a fair amount of AT&T stock from the employee investment plan which guided her into a comfortable retirement. She felt rich as a result of what Father Kelly and AT&T had done for her.

Mammy continued to live at the Cortelyou Road apartment we had acquired following numerous moves from Jefferson Avenue, to Halsey Street, to Ralph Avenue, to Atlantic Avenue in

Queens, back to Brooklyn's East New York on Cleveland Street, and finally to Cortelyou Road in Brooklyn's Flatbush area. The nearby Erasmus Hall High School offered evening courses for those seeking a high school diploma, and with my sister Helen's encouragement, Mammy enrolled in Erasmus with the goal of obtaining her high school equivalency degree. In Ireland, she'd gotten only a fourth-grade education, yet she read voraciously and loved writing. I recall her often reciting entire sections of Coleridge's *The Rime of the Ancient Mariner* by heart. She did well at Erasmus. However, the growing crime menace of the area ended her studies. The Flatbush neighborhood became another Jefferson Avenue, a neighborhood in transition, with crime becoming more and more common.

On exiting the school on Church Avenue one night, Mammy saw five teens approaching her. Sensing she was about to be mugged, she threw her pocketbook across the street and the felons went for it as she ran the other way. Her apartment became an armed fortress, with three locks on the front door, and the back windows nailed shut. To enter the place became an ordeal since she had to remove a chain as well as open the locks to allow any of us to enter! Breaking into Fort Knox would have been less challenging.

She finally became convinced to move out of Brooklyn to a senior citizen complex in Keyport, New Jersey near my sister Bunny's family. When

Bunny moved to Florida, Mammy followed to a complex in West Palm Beach. This didn't last more than three years since, again, crime became an issue. She claimed, "You couldn't go out in the daytime because of the heat, and you couldn't go out at night because of the criminals." (West Palm Beach, then and now, has a high crime rate, and in the late 1980s it was in the Top Ten Crime Cities in the USA). When Mammy moved to Pasadena, California, close to Helen's family, she loved her apartment, the great climate, and the relatively crime-free environment, and she remained there until her death in 1992. Quite an odyssey — from The Glen in County Derry to the streets of Brooklyn to the affluent suburbs of New Jersey and California. As my sister Helen would remind me, she became "a California gal at last!"

A few words about my grandmother Tilda, "Granny," will round out my account. Without her, any semblance of a normal family life would have been impossible. Since my mom worked nights, generally from 11 p.m. to 7 a.m., Granny cared for us, watched us, protected us, and disciplined us, often with a leather strap. With hindsight I realize what a difficult task she had and how remarkably well she helped in raising us. Yet economic and physical problems abounded. Since Granny had no financial resources whatsoever, her care increasingly strained our limited family budget. To remedy this, Mammy, my Uncle Frank and a family friend,

Johnny Mullan, wondered if Tilda could qualify for Social Security benefits. They commissioned me to go to our local Democratic assemblyman's office to find out. Tilly announced, "James, you're the man of the house. Go to Travia's office and see what you can get." Wow! Here I was age fifteen, sent off to speak to the Honorable Anthony Travia, the district leader of the 46th N.Y. State Assembly District!

So one evening I ventured to Travia's office a few blocks away from our Cleveland Street apartment in Brooklyn's East New York neighborhood. There I encountered an elderly grizzled aide, typical of the Tammany Hall cronies of that era. He stared at me coldly. "What do you want here?" he snapped. I told him why I'd come and he curtly told me to wait on the bench with the other supplicants seeking favors.

In those days in Brooklyn you went to the local Democratic district office to seek help when needed. Tammany Hall, the New York Democratic organization, frequently provided all sorts of aid to those in need: if your kid had been arrested, you asked the Democratic politicians to help with his release; if you were down-and-out, Tammany Hall provided you with a turkey at Christmas or, in earlier times, a bucket of coal; if you were unemployed the organization provided a temporary job such as shoveling snow or delivering mail during the Christmas holidays. Direct personalized service was the norm, and the only thing asked of those receiving assistance was to "vote Democratic in November," which all my family did. Few Republicans ever had a chance running against the Democratic "machine." Tilly always reminded us that the Democrats were for the common people like us. The Republicans were for the rich. (However, she sheepishly admitted years later that she voted for Eisenhower for president since he had been a good general during the war. His opponent, Adlai Stevenson, was too aloof in her opinion).

When my turn came, I entered Travia's office. An impressive, polite, well-dressed man, Travia listened to my inquiry. He took extensive notes on Granny's immigration and work history and said he would look into the matter and that I should return in two weeks. He did add that he doubted that anything could be done about Social Security since Granny had not been gainfully employed since 1935 when the Social Security benefits became law. Two weeks later I returned and encountered the same irritable aide who said, "You again. What do you want this time?" After explaining my return, I was sent to another aide who told me unfortunately nothing could be done because Granny hadn't worked since 1935—just as Mr. Travia had thought. Well, at least we tried. I certainly was thankful for Travia's efforts and definitely would have voted for him if I'd been old enough. He eventually became the Speaker of the New York State Assembly and later a federal judge in the

United States Eastern District of New York. Although he couldn't deliver what we sought, even today I have fond memories of him.

As my grandmother aged, she developed a multitude of medical problems: a heart condition, diabetes, and rheumatoid arthritis. By the time my sisters and I reached adolescence, she had become a total invalid, an increasing burden to all of us. My mom and sisters bore most of this burden. By 1958 Grammy's physical condition had deteriorated dramatically. Yet she refused to be hospitalized. Never in her life had she been hospitalized. She always claimed that being committed to a hospital was "going to the poor house" which in the Ireland of her youth was indeed the case. In early twentieth century Ireland, one went to the hospital to die, not to get better from an ailment.

Dr. George Bodkin, our family physician, finally intervened. On one of his family house calls, he pulled me aside and said, "You're the man of the house now. You have one of two choices—either your grandmother has to go to the hospital, or your mother will drop dead from the stress of caring for her. It's up to you since your mother seems incapable of telling her mother she has to be hospitalized."

I made the decision and told Mammy that Granny had to go, that there was no other alternative. Mammy very reluctantly consented and Granny went by ambulance to Kings County Hospital.

There she refused to eat or even speak to us, so furious was she that we'd sent her there against her will. Sadly, she lasted only two weeks and died there from her heart condition. (Or was it a broken heart?) She was eighty-seven years old.

Soon after her death we made the funeral arrangements. The family delegated me—"the reluctant man of the house"—to go to the local funeral home to organize the wake and the funeral Mass and purchase the casket. Uncle Dan, my father's younger brother, accompanied me. Dan left Ireland in his late thirties, only a year before Granny's death.

When we arrived, the funeral director ushered us into The Casket Room to pick a coffin. Of course the director, with a feigned sorrowful look, directed our attention to the most expensive casket. "Naturally you would want the best for Mrs. Mullin. She should be buried in a fine casket such as this one, befitting her true dignity."

Uncle Dan snapped, "Enough of your blathering nonsense. How much money are you making on this casket? This lad's poor mother is a widow raising three young ones. We're not interested in your soaking and cheating us like you do to the other poor fools who come here with you preying on their grief. Show us your cheapest casket since the poor woman wouldn't have cared a bit what she was buried in!"

I was aghast!

Then Uncle Dan started bargaining over a coffin, cajoling the director, even threatening to leave and arrange the funeral elsewhere.

I was completely stunned. Who ever bargains for a coffin?

The director, horrified and clearly intimidated by Uncle Dan (who could easily terrify any adversary) quickly showed us a more reasonable model and even lowered its price substantially.

The deal done, we left with Uncle Dan elated and me shell-shocked over the encounter.

We waked Granny in the funeral parlor and buried her in St. John's Cemetery in Queens, following her Mass at St. Michael's Church on Jerome Street. Immediately after the interment, most of our relatives and friends returned to our Cleveland Street apartment, sad over the loss of Granny. But Irish traditions persisted and Joe McCloskey, one of my mom's fellow Irish immigrant friends, announced in our living room, "Tilda would not be pleased with us all looking glum and so sad." Then he pulled out his accordion and started playing Irish reels, shouting to me, "James, go to the local gin mill and get some beer and whiskey for us. Tilda would be happy knowing that we're having a good time in her honor."

Aghast again, I did what he commanded and obtained the whiskey and beer even though legally

I never should have since I was only sixteen years old. All of us became less dejected. Though at first I worried that what we were doing might be sacrilegious, ultimately we had a rollicking good time. But that's how the Irish then celebrated both life and death. At peace in heaven, Tilda would appreciate our celebrating her passing to a better life, not bemoaning her absence. You might have to be Irish to understand that "ah, it's a far better life that she's off to."

This event recalls an earlier episode. Let me go off on a slight tangent here to alert you to additional aspects of Irish culture. My Granny's cousin, Aunt Kate, lived with her husband Charlie Mullan on Linden Street in the Bushwick section, a few blocks away from Jefferson Avenue. Granny and Mammy would often visit them and I enjoyed going there since Aunt Kate always gave me beer, sometimes even whiskey, even when I was only seven or eight years old. Aunt Kate usually sat in a large rocking chair, next to which stood an open quart bottle of Rheingold beer which she "sipped" throughout the day. Whenever we visited, she would give me a small glass of the brew. "Here James, here's a wee bit of beer for you. Swallow it and get rid of your terrible thirst." Mammy always worried that this might not be a good idea since I might develop a taste for alcohol at such a young age. "Ah, shut up, Tilly, the drink will do him good." Kate and Charlie's middle-aged single nephew, Johnny McKinney (my godfather's brother), lived in the same apartment, and Aunt Kate would tell him, "Johnny, you skittery old bag, take the wee ones for some ice cream." To our delight, he always did. When we would finally leave Kate's place at the end of the afternoon, she and Uncle Charlie and Johnny always gave me a "wee penny," usually a dollar or more. Again, this was for my mother, but never so stated, preserving Tilly's dignity and sense of honor.

When Uncle Charlie died at age eighty, Aunt Kate actually waked him in their Linden Street apartment, the last wake or viewing I ever attended in a house. The new custom dating from the early 1950s dictated that Irish wakes be held in the more dignified setting of the funeral parlor. Its posh chairs, heavy drapery, and thick carpets lent an air of dignity and sobriety befitting the recent upward mobility of the Irish Americans. The funeral parlor illustrated the transition from the "shanty Irish" to the "lace curtain Irish." I guess today we would have to add the "picture window Irish!" (Or would it be the "Venetian blinds Irish" or "window treatment Irish?")

I vividly remember the event. As we entered Aunt Kate's apartment, Mammy directed my sisters and me straight to the front bedroom where Uncle Charlie's corpse lay on his bed surrounded by lighted candles, holy pictures with palm branches behind them, a crucifix, and a few flowers. There we knelt and prayed for his soul. (I did check his chest to make sure he wasn't breathing and not in any danger of being buried alive.) Then we proceeded to the kitchen where dozens of mourners were eating, drinking, and boisterously socializing. Aunt Kate mingled amongst them. Mammy, as well as every mourner, said the same thing to her, "Kate, I'm sorry for your troubles." True to the traditions of the Irish wake, all had a pleasant time, honoring Charlie, now freed from life's toils and finally residing in Paradise. Americanization has taken its toll on the Irish wake. I think we've lost something precious regarding the way life and death are viewed. Largely stripped of their ultimate meanings, sanitized in the funeral parlor with its somber, depressing, colorless atmosphere, Irish wakes and funerals aren't the same. Yet as late as the mid-1970s, a remnant remained. When my wife Marge and I attended the wake of Uncle Eddy Donaghy in a Bronx funeral parlor on Fordham Road, I saw a sign on the wall which read "POSITIVELY NO EATING OR DRINKING PERMITTED IN THE MAIN PARLOR!" Alas! How times change. I might note that the sign also was translated into Spanish for the sake of (or warning to) Latino mourners.

The North Side of Jefferson Avenue

Before I get too involved with the happenings on Jefferson Avenue and the adjacent streets, let me describe the actual block (refer to the maps in the Appendix on page 198). My old neighborhood occupied a fairly sizeable section of northeast Brooklyn in the Bedford-Stuyvesant section. Nearby, the Bushwick section began on the other side of Broadway, the main avenue over which the tracks of the Jamaica El (elevated train) ran. To the west lay the Williamsburg and Fort Greene sections; to the east were the East New York and Oceanhill-Brownsville sections. Some purists say that Bedford-Stuyvesant only comprised the area between Bedford and Stuyvesant avenues, but just about everyone believed it stretched to Broadway where the Bushwick neighborhood began. The focal point of my early life was the section of Jefferson Avenue close to the end of the Bed-Stuy area.

Physically, Jefferson Avenue remains scarcely different than it appeared sixty years ago. Naturally, individual structures evidence changes, some with major renovations, some with noticeable deterioration, most with only minor cosmetic modifications. Today's block remains substantially similar to my memory of it, aside from the trees now lining Jefferson Avenue. What has changed is my current awareness of how small Jefferson Avenue actually is, as opposed to my childhood recollection of its immensity. Back then its length between Ralph and Howard Avenues seemed limitless. Presumably, all of us have similar memories of how large everything appeared in our childhood, from our homes and apartments to our neighborhoods, towns, schools, parks, and playgrounds.

Our part of Jefferson Avenue housed approximately thirty three-story apartment buildings on each side, mostly brownstones. This meant that more than two hundred families, with about eight hundred people, lived on Jefferson. That explains why there were at least thirty children (and friends) my own age living on that single street and running amok between the borders of Ralph and Howard avenues.

In the 1950s, the residents of our street assumed a larger-than-life quality, some colorful, some despicable, some gracious and friendly, some blank slates leaving no permanent impact on my psyche. In my mind's eye I can still see many of them as I tour Jefferson Avenue and reimagine the houses and characters who inhabited the center of my universe.

My tour begins at the northwest corner of Jefferson and Ralph Avenues, the outer limit of my childhood world. There stood the local bar, the well-named Glow Tavern and Grill. The Glow exemplified the typical Irish saloon of that era though the owners may have been Jewish! It was sparsely furnished with a long beat-up bar surrounded by equally decrepit bar stools. A well-kept shuffle board, across from the bar, basked under a solitary green fluorescent light fixture. A full-length wall mirror hung behind the bar and underneath it stood a counter well stocked with bottles of gin, Scotch, and Irish and American whiskeys. The grill part of the Glow's name certainly would perplex any patron seeking a meal therein, since food actually never appeared at the Glow except for a few bowls of peanuts and pretzels, heavily salted to encourage copious drinking by those assembled.

Like most saloons, the Glow also boasted a back section with a few tables and chairs, ostensibly there for those who might wish to feast on the saloon's nonexistent meals. One could enter this "dining room" either from the bar area itself or from the separate street entrance on Jefferson Avenue. Outside that entrance door a sign read, "LADIES INVITED," which, of course, signified the exact opposite. Females rarely appeared in the Glow and those reputable Irish ladies who did so were seated in this separate section, always accompanied by either their husbands or immediate family members. Any females venturing into the actual bar area, the inner sanctum of male bonding, would immediately have their honor and virtue questioned throughout the neighborhood, and they'd be castigated as bar flies and local drunks.

The Glow exhibited no Irish flags, no Easter Sunday Rising posters, no pictures whatsoever, not even a television set until the mid-1950s. Its trappings could only be described "Brooklyn austere." Saturday night brawls were not uncommon, though these later became rare as the Irish sought to move up the social ladder by emulating the much more refined and civilized manners of the WASP middle class to which they generally aspired. Gradually, the Irish gained "couth and culture" and the Glow-type rough and ready Irish bars and grills disappeared from the urban landscape, replaced by the chic, trendy Irish taverns that now populate many urban gentrified neighborhoods, all claiming to be authentically Irish. While they lasted, these old Glow saloons served as neighborhood meeting places for Irish conviviality where men could congregate to argue politics, discuss baseball, celebrate their triumphs, or drown their sorrows in their beer or whiskey. The bartender would dole out one drink free of charge after the purchase of three drinks, the generous "buy back" of any respectable saloon. Lax in the observance of legal codes, the Glows of Brooklyn would often serve minors, no questions asked, to which I can attest from experience.

In the spring of 1950 my family hosted a party in our apartment to celebrate the arrival of Father McKenna, a priest relative, from Ireland. My uncles commissioned me to go to the Glow to obtain a pail of beer—yes, you actually brought your own pail or bucket to the bar—which I dutifully did. I believe I was nine years old at that time. Were that to occur today, the bar would be bolted shut, its owners arrested, fined, and possibly jailed, and the young "victim" would be put up for adoption and probably be the subject of a 10 p.m. news investigative report detailing the corruption lurking not far beneath the surface in the urban demimonde. Alas, how times change.

We now leave the Glow Tavern to continue our virtual tour of the block. Peter Fiorillo's apartment house loomed next to the Glow on my mental map of the north side of Jefferson Avenue. Peter and I always played together as children and I consider him to be one of my earliest and closest friends on the street. From Peter, I learned two mind-boggling facts—that Italians actually existed and that they lived very differently than we Irish.

First, they ate pasta every day and never ate potatoes. How could anyone eat that much spaghetti and avoid life's most gratifying food, the magnificent, all-purpose potato? Over the next few years, new shocks in the form of pizza, tortellini, and calamari assaulted my refined food sensibilities, previously accustomed only to potatoes, chicken, Del Monte peas and carrots, and the occasional turnip. But after a while, accommodate we did. On Friday nights my mother would serve an Italian meal which my grandmother, my two younger sisters, and I termed Irish spaghetti: Mueller's spaghetti covered with Hunt's tomato sauce and Borden cheddar cheese grated extra fine to enhance the exquisite culinary experience.

Second, Peter's family Sunday dinner would take several hours to consume. An entire afternoon was almost completely wasted as I waited for him to finish and come out to play. We Irish would wolf down our meal, sometimes even standing, as we raced to finish and return to the street. Irish cooking could never be considered haute cuisine, so all the better that you consumed it quickly and got the necessary ordeal over with. But in Peter's case, I encountered the wall of the Great Italian Dinner Ritual! Each time I rang Peter's bell, his mother responded that he was still eating and I should come back later. Returning an hour later, she repeated her response. A further two hours would elapse before Peter finally emerged, stuffed but ready to play. What could he possibly be eating? But by that time I had often become faint with hunger myself and in my famished state returned to my home for refueling. Just as I could not fathom how anyone could spend three hours eating, Peter could scarcely believe that we Irish could eat so hurriedly, unwilling and incapable of enjoying our meal. No wonder we Irish looked so skinny! Peter also could not believe that I enjoyed eating sugar sandwiches. At a recent reunion of our gang, he reminded everyone that I would take a piece of white bread, pour sugar on it, fold it, and eat it. Since the sugar often fell off the bread, he recalled that I eventually started spreading the bread with warm butter (to which the sugar stuck). Folding it like a taco shell, I then consumed it, relishing every moment of ritual. Sixty years later, I'm surprised I'm not diabetic.

It was my friendship with Peter which slowly prepared me for my exposure to Brooklyn's "multiculturalism," a theme and a reality so prevalent today but one that no one had ever heard of in my childhood. For most of my life I erroneously believed that Jefferson Avenue harbored mainly the

Irish. Yet as I calculate the perceived ethnic composition of my block in the late 1940s and early 1950s, I now realize the Italians comprised the largest single ethnic group. My friends' names were Peter Fiorillo, Paulie Azzarra, Joey Mazolla, and Louie Mione.

The Italians had arrived on the block in the late 1940s. As these newcomers moved in, many old-timers believed that they would be murdered in their beds, with their throats slit with that most popular Italian weapon—the stiletto. One had best sleep lightly so as to avoid falling prey to a Sicilian assassin! The next wave comprised the blacks, or African Americans, as they are currently called. As they arrived on Jefferson Avenue, new fears emerged as the Irish, Germans, Jews, and their new comrades, the Italians, convinced themselves that this new group would murder them with their preferred weapon of choice, the switchblade knife. More sleepless nights! By the mid- to late-1950s, the Puerto Ricans began to arrive en masse, creating even greater fears. Now the Irish, Germans, Jews, Italians, and African Americans panicked at the thought of being murdered in their beds by a Puerto Rican yielding a machete who would gleefully hack them to death while muttering unintelligible Hispanic gibberish!

Of course, we youngsters eventually realized that no one had actually been sliced, stabbed, or hacked by anyone else, and we gradually acclimated to each other. Our "gang" could be said to be fully integrated and ethnicity mattered little, except in the ethnic jokes we constantly leveled at each other, though always in a friendly, non-humiliating way. But even this ethnic mix gradually changed in the 1950s as new groups moved onto Jefferson Avenue, replacing and succeeding the older Irish, German, and Jewish groups who began escaping to that unknown realm known as "the country" — that is, the vast hinterland far away in Long Island.

Next stop on our virtual tour, we come to the apartment house where lived a suspected child molester or such was the gossip in our street. Like all the mothers on the block, Mammy admonished my sisters and me to never linger near that house and under all circumstances never speak to him. I never did. "Don't you even look at him!" she said. Come to think of it, I never set eyes on the man and had no real idea who he was. Apparently, he had a family with several daughters, but their family never mixed with anyone else on Jefferson Avenue. Perhaps unfairly, the family was considered "riff-raff" and miscreants to be avoided at any cost— even though no one ever expressly stated, or even seemed to know, just what it was that the pervert father supposedly had done. The rumor seemed to have a life of its own, which was not uncommon on Jefferson Avenue. Fortunately, before the mothers of our street marched on his building with flaming torches, the man and his family moved to "the country," where everyone who left Jefferson Avenue seemed to relocate, and the problem was solved.

Two buildings down from the alleged pervert lived Mrs. Marie Behan, together with her daughter Dolores, and her son John who then served in the army during the Korean War. Mrs. Behan loved life and enjoyed it to the full. At almost 300 pounds, she enjoyed eating, drinking, dancing, and socializing. The life of any family party or social gathering, she could be labeled a complete extrovert, whose hilarious sense of humor and foul-mouthed tongue would demolish any challenger. Self-giving and generous as she was, our family could always depend on her. Following the death of my father in 1944, Mrs. Behan helped us in immeasurable ways, assisting my mother and caring for my elderly infirm grandmother. Neighbors such as Mrs. Behan helped us move on in life at a time when few financial or social resources existed to assist us.

My sisters and I are indebted to Mrs. Behan for possibly saving our mom's life. Turns out that my mother developed an allergy to penicillin and was unaware of how dangerous this could be when she had taken medicine containing it. On that day, Mrs. Behan visited, took one look at her, and exclaimed to my mom that she should immediately see a doctor. "Tilly," she said, "you'll die and who will raise your three kids?" She summoned a doctor, thus averting a possible catastrophe. There's a special place in heaven for her.

Her daughter Dolores, a few years older than I, helped tutor me in the intricacies of long division, multiplying fractions, and other mysteries of what we then termed arithmetic. Were it not for her patient efforts I'm sure I'd have been a grade school dropout consigned eternally to the ranks of the numerically challenged. Without Dolores's assistance I never would have advanced to the Pythagorean Theorem or the calculations of a square root.

Dolores's older brother John served in Korea and returned on leave for a few weeks. On the day of his return, I excitedly visited their apartment and pumped John with all sorts of questions about the army. Did he kill any commies? What was it like in a foxhole near the Chinese border? Did he bayonet any North Koreans? He politely ignored my queries and reminded me that he served in the artillery, miles behind the front lines.

Like all families the Behans suffered their share of tragedy: Mrs. Behan's husband John Sr. was accidentally but seriously wounded by a New York City police officer. He served as a transit officer (the police for the New York subway system) and, in a case of mistaken identity, had been shot in an encounter at a subway station in East New York. Fortunately, he survived. In spite of this personal tragedy, Mrs. Behan never wavered in providing help to others, and the simple fact is that we could scarcely have survived without her.

Tragedy seemed to pervade the apartment house in which the Behans resided. Her landlady, who lived on the third floor, fell to her death as she slipped out her kitchen window while hanging her wash on the backyard clothesline. Her death shocked the street and reminded everyone of the fragility of life. You're alive one moment, and then lying dead in a backyard the next. I remember little about the poor woman, not even her name, yet the manner and circumstance of her death remain with me almost six decades later. I do recall that the poor landlady's grandson, Allan Dale, a famous singer, had once visited her house on Jefferson Avenue. His songs always made The Hit Parade, including "Cherry Pink and Apple Blossom White" and "The Gang That Sang Heart of My Heart." The entire block greeted him, the girls went wild meeting the "Prince of Crooners," and they all demanded his autograph. At the time I was only ten and could only wonder what all the fuss was about.

Three doors down the street lived the Taylors, the first African American family I was to meet. Friendly and gregarious, the Taylors mixed well with my sisters and me. Wilbur, Jennifer and Jean Taylor often played with us, and I think fondly of them still.

Wilbur was quite an athlete. Often our group would play a game — Three Steps Over Germany —

with one kid in the middle of the street, who was "IT." The other players would stand on the sidewalk and each had three free jumps to get across, past "IT." Then the jumper had to stand still; if he moved even so slightly, he then was tagged by another player and became "IT." Wilbur was so athletic that he crossed the entire street in his three jumps. As Pete Fiorillo reminded me recently, "That ended that game!"

As an aside, I frequently visit Jefferson Avenue on my Drew University criminology class "tours" of Bedford-Stuyvesant, a field trip examining drug supermarkets, murder scenes, and vigilante actions. Occasionally when our bus has stopped on Jefferson Avenue, I've inquired of the current residents as to the whereabouts of the Taylors, particularly Wilbur. They've told me that the Taylors still live there, but that they haven't yet come home from their jobs. My trip to the street takes place in the early afternoon. Hopefully, we will meet again.

The Passalaquas lived next door to the Taylors. The family had three daughters roughly the same age as my sisters and I. I tried to avoid the sisters, because they were girls, a species to be ignored and avoided whenever possible. The Passalaquas certainly were a fine family yet I have one thing against their daughters, particularly the oldest, Frances. One summer's day, the three of them and my sisters decided the time had come to introduce me to the delicious wonder of tomatoes, which they

Collection of James M. O'Kane

With my sisters: Bernadette (Bunny), me, and Helen (1945).

knew I hated. They held me down while Frances forced a tomato sandwich into my mouth; I can still work up a nauseous response if I dwell on the villainous act! To this day I still loathe tomatoes as well as most other fruits and vegetables, though inexplicably I love tomato sauce and tomato juice.

The next stop in this Jefferson Avenue odyssey is 899 Jefferson Avenue, the center of my childhood world. Here I lived with my mother, my grandmother, and my two sisters Helen and Bunny. We lived in the second-floor apartment of a three apartment building. Upstairs lived Mrs. Hill, an elderly Jewish lady crippled with arthritis, and her daughter Agnes. Friendly but reserved, Mrs. Hill and my mother often chatted, usually complaining about the landlord Mr. Paolocci, who lived on the first floor. He constantly complained about the noise my sisters and I made, most notably centering on the one time we chose to skate (with actual steel roller skates) in our apartment. Why someone would complain about such a wholesome, playful occasion baffled me.

Thankfully, the Saeta family purchased 899 in 1949. An Italian couple with a boy my age, Charlie, the Saetas initially scared me because they were Italian. True, other Italians lived on our street, but these Italians lived in my house! I certainly didn't want to live THAT close to them. Visions of them knifing me in my bed took over my dreams, or shall we say, nightmares. Yet my fears never materialized since their son Charlie and I became good friends and frequently played together along with Peter Fiorillo as well as Albert Filosa and his sister Marilyn, who lived two doors up the street. I was surrounded by Italians. I remember little about Albert because he and his family soon moved to "the country" of Long Island, as did Joey Stalzer, another friend who lived just three houses down from 899. What terrible crime had they committed to be sentenced to suburbia so young? Why had they been forced to take the GI Bill mortgages which sealed their doom in the country?

Other characters abounded in our area. Across the backyard of 899 Jefferson, in the houses on Putnam, lived a World War I shell-shocked veteran whom everyone called The Shadow (named for the pulp fiction comic book hero and radio favorite, Lamont Cranston. We all know the answer to "who knows what evil lurks in the hearts of men?" And we could all shout, "The Shadow knows!"). Harmless, but quite psychotic, the ex-soldier would occasionally race around his backyard completely naked until his wife could calm him and get him inside. Well liked by her neighbors, the Shadow's wife would feed all the stray cats in the area, daily pouring out a pot of hot oatmeal for them. Literally, you could count thirty to forty cats partaking of this feast every morning. Even my cat Hitler joined in on the free breakfast.

One big problem: as Pat Connelly recently reminded me, the cats stayed around, and nightly the neighbors were subjected to cat fights, screams, screeches, and mating calls, so much so that some of The Shadow's neighbors took matters into their own hands. A few of them lured the cats into a nearby cellar with enticements of food and milk, and then shot them with .22 caliber pistols. I always thought this showed how crazy and demented some of the locals could be, and I always wondered if a serial killer or two, like Ted Bundy or Jeffrey Dahmer, might have been among the vigilantes. You know this is how they start, torturing and killing small animals.

But back to Jefferson Avenue. The next building housed the Fanelli family. The Fanellis had two sons—Vincent, and an older brother Sean. It was Sean who eventually had an illustrious career as the president of a local community college. Every summer his mom would pack up the entire family for a full summer vacation on Long Island. At the time I regarded this as a sad fate for Vincent and Sean. Today, though, I admire what his mom did for all the Fanellis. Vincent and I often played together until, predictably, he and his family moved away, not to the country, but to the Flatbush section of Brooklyn where I visited him a few times. His new home bordered one of the two indoor roller skating rinks which I thought most impressive. I still recall skating there to the sound of a barely functional organ piping out "Lady of Spain" as older teenage security personnel with very impressive armbands kept the flow of skaters moving in the proper direction, always counterclockwise.

The growing exodus to "the country" unsettled most of my permanent playmates. Who would want to live far away from a neighborhood teeming with kids? How would they survive amidst all that fresh air, grass, and trees? Once more the GI Bill mortgage rates were at work.

On two separate miserable occasions I, too, suffered a similar, but fortunately temporary, exile. The well-meaning church ladies of Our Lady of Good Counsel parish thought it would be a grand idea to send me to St. Vincent de Paul summer camp in Commack, Long Island so as to give my poor mother a brief respite. Deeply ambivalent about the whole idea, she eventually agreed and off to camp I went, spending two weeks there during two successive summers—miserable, lonely, and very homesick. I hoped I would contract polio, thus sparing me this ordeal, and I actually prayed for the disease. Fortunately, my prayers went unanswered.

The nuns who ran the camp were actually quite nurturing and caring, though one elderly German nun was rumored to have been undoubtedly a Nazi prison guard in her previous life. She insisted on running the camp as a benevolent concentration camp. At night, she would inspect our dorm, flashing a light on everyone's face to make sure we were all asleep. If not, she screamed, "Get to sleep," thus waking up those already sleeping. During lunch one afternoon, we were served a salad with lettuce, tomatoes, and mayonnaise, all of which I detested. She told me to sit there and not leave the table until I ate it, which I simply could not. All the other six-year-old boys tramped off to their naps while I sat alone having no idea what to do, quietly whimpering over my fate. Along came two teenage busboys cleaning the tables. One asked me what was wrong. I related my sad tale and he responded, "Here, throw it in the garbage." I looked at him, but then I did, and I was startled as to how easily my problem resolved itself. I returned to my dorm for my nap, telling Sister Nazi that I had indeed finished my lunch. Over sixty years later, I still harbor serious guilt over these monumental transgressions of throwing away my salad and lying to a nun!

The following summer saw a repeat of the camp disaster when the well-meaning church ladies sent me back to St. Vincent's. But this time I was accompanied by my sister Helen. Both she and I hated the camp and actually plotted to run away and take a taxi back to Brooklyn. We could see the highway beyond the potato field bordering St. Vincent's and thought if we could cross that field, we could grab a cab or at worst walk home to Jefferson Avenue (probably about forty miles away), but we knew we weren't allowed to cross any street with traffic on it, let alone a highway, so our plan had to be aborted. When I did return home from that POW experience, my friends greeted me warmly and wondered how I had survived. They considered themselves fortunate indeed that they'd not been sent there, away from their Brooklyn summer vacation. We agreed that it was best for all concerned to avoid any future offers from Good Counsel's church ladies. Who knew where else they might send us?

Johnny Schumaker, one of the older boys on Jefferson Avenue, also moved to the "country" and it was obvious that neighbors were dropping like flies! Then came Mario Abuzzo's house. (His real name, like some on our tour, has been altered so as to protect the guilty.) Mario and I simply rubbed each other the wrong way, as did his mother and my mom. Fights on Jefferson Avenue frequently took place, and he and I tangled often; sometimes I won, sometimes he did. On one occasion he did a job on me, and I ran crying to my mother who immediately confronted his mother. I still recall the screaming match. Thinking we were German, Mario's mother yelled at us, "Go back to Hitler," to which my mom retorted, "You go back to Mussolini!" (The reader should know that this encounter occurred only a few years after the end of World War II, and stuffed effigies of Hitler and Mussolini still hung from street lights on the block.) Eventually things did settle down, the normal course of neighborhood street life reasserted itself, and Mario and I grudgingly accommodated each other's existence.

Billy Ritchie's apartment comes next on our trip down Jefferson Avenue. His family became a local legend because they purchased the very first television on the street, which created quite a stir. My friends and I believed Billy to be fantastically rich since his parents could afford this new novelty. Maybe it had something to do with his last name. With decades of hindsight, of course I now view the Ritchies as a typical normal family who were not particularly affluent. Billy's father, I believe, drove a trolley car for the Transit Authority — not a profession associated with enormous wealth. Nevertheless, Billy flaunted his TV set as an effective status symbol. I believe it was a twelve-inch circular screen Zenith. His apartment occupied the first floor of a three-story building, so we could stand on his stoop and look through his living room window and actually watch TV! We did this often, clustering close to the window to watch the *Howdy Doody Show* if Billy allowed it. Generally he was quite generous, allowing us this great privilege, but every so often he would close the curtain in front of the window, blocking our view, the ultimate weapon in the never-ending game of one-upmanship wherein his peer group humbly accepted its secondary status. But Billy never pushed things too far, and on several occasions I, and presumably others, benefited from our friendship with him and actually were invited <u>into</u> his home to view magic TV. He stands high in my pecking order of notable characters on the block. Alas, he also soon thereafter made the move from Jefferson Avenue, with his TV, also presumably to the distant potato fields of Long Island, banished forever from all the amenities of Brooklyn life. Fortunately other TVs soon began sprouting on our block, so Billy's exile to "the country" quickly faded from our group's consciousness, especially when we heard that color TVs were coming. Wow! Well, sort of. The father of one of my friends (I can't remember which one) actually bought a "converter," which turned out to be a piece of clear plastic the size of the standard twelve-inch TV screen of the day. It had three horizontal bands tinted in red, yellow, and green. He taped it over their family's black and white TV screen and, *voilà*, color TV! Well, sort of. I believe that piece of plastic lasted less than a week because everyone in the house was getting seasick watching the professional wrestlers through the stupid thing. Imagine Mad Mountain Dean colored green.

Our tour now takes us to perhaps the most colorful character on the street—"Bopsy" or "Bop" Jones. Bop lived next door to Billy Ritchie and he mixed with everyone. Funny, unpredictable, truly impulsive and somewhat scatterbrained, Bop lived 24/7 on the street, always eager to play and "goof off" with anyone available. Yet you couldn't push Bop too far since he had a short fuse and could lash out at the slightest provocation even though he was short and skinny and couldn't fight his way out of a paper bag. His fighting ability put him at the bottom of the block's macho pecking order. His temper reached legendary status at his ninth birthday party, to which almost the entire block of kids (boys only) were invited. Things moved quite smoothly at the party until something happened. Perhaps another kid insulted Bop. Incensed, he picked up his beautifully decorated birthday cake, ran to the window, and threw it into the backyard. His mother screamed! We didn't even have time to blow out the candles and open his presents because he threw all of us out of his apartment as well. We ran into other kids who were just arriving. What a surprise for them.

For the next two weeks, we never saw Bop, but he finally emerged and acted as if nothing had happened. Eventually he laughed with us about his memorable celebration, the only birthday party of which I have any recollection. As Peter Fiorillo recently reminded me, we all probably had birthday parties but neither of us could remember any of them other than Bop's.

Fast forward to Bop's teenage years. He traveled to a gypsy tattoo parlor in Coney Island to have his left ankle tattooed with an expression I'd like to omit from this account. I'll give you some clues: The expression consisted of an imperative. The first word contained four letters. The second word spelled Y-O-U. Bop delighted in lifting his trouser leg to display his creation, particularly to elderly women. As the novelty of Bop's tattoo faded, his embarrassment over it mounted, particularly when our group ventured to the beach at Coney Island. Often he would refuse to strip to his bathing suit, claiming that the weather was too chilly to do so—even when the temperatures hovered around 96 degrees. Finally he solved his dilemma by returning to the gypsies and having them embellish his tattoo with flowers, fierce eagles, and patriotic phrases that covered the original words.

In his apartment building lived the Williams family, with Rita and Rosemary, but since they were girls I paid little heed to them. Ah, what a mistake since both, particularly Rita, were beautiful. Next door to Bop lived a truly despicable man loathed by all in my group, and probably by most of the residents of Jefferson Avenue. Let's call him Mr. Heinz. Little was known about Heinz, other than the fact that he immigrated from Germany. He obviously hated children, never missing an opportunity to harass us from his second-floor window where he sat, perpetually chewing tobacco and spitting the residue into a tin can. When we would pass by, he would curse and spit at us and on many occasions try to douse us with the can's contents. Imagine being hit with that mixture! Our gang rarely backed down from such encounters and we returned his insults, throwing snowballs at him in winter and calling him a Nazi, which we had no doubt he was. This, of course, only agitated what might have been his inner demons, but it pleased us immensely as we imagined that we were fighting a member of Hitler's inner circle hiding in his pathetic bunker on Jefferson Avenue. We told each other he probably had the misfortune of missing the last German submarine to Argentina, ending up in his last choice destination, Jefferson Avenue! Perhaps we should have contacted the FBI about Heinz, but no one thought of it at the time. The Gestapo would have been honored to have him in their ranks.

The next few houses, all nicely appointed brownstones, remain mainly a blank in my mind. I believe all were owned by their residents, and few of them had children, although none my age. However, a few memories stand out.

In the first house lived Mr. and Mrs. Brady, an elderly childless Irish couple, very prim and proper. In warm weather they sat in their front yard watching the perpetual action on the street. Quite fond of my sisters and me, they never ceased to invite us to sit and chat with them as we tried to sneak past their house. We dreaded such encounters since the ensuing conversations bored us to death. Now I realize the couple probably was quite lonely, but at that time we couldn't wait to leave and feigned some feeble excuse to exit their yard. Sixty years later I still remain guilt-ridden over my poor behavior, embarrassed by my do-we-have-to-sit-and-talk-to-the-old-people attitude.

Two doors down from the Brady's lived a truly interesting African American lady, middle-aged, charming, and very self-assured. Apparently she had been an opera singer and everything about her suggested theatrical excess. She dressed in flamboyant, colorful dresses and coats and always donned a brightly colored turban. Bedecked with large hoop earrings and numerous rings and bracelets, she mesmerized the block. Confident and outgoing, she rarely spoke to me or my riffraff friends. She never really mixed with any of Jefferson Avenue's residents, but we all held her in awe, particularly my sisters who even now view her as a positive trendsetter, a feminist before feminism became fashionable. I never learned her name or anything substantive about her, but I am convinced she played the leading roles in *Carmen* and *Aida* somewhere, a virtual prima donna living in our midst.

Her brownstone's stairs to the building's second floor became one of our gang's favorite places from which we unleashed havoc on passing motorists. Since she "went to business" daily, we had free reign of that second-floor landing to which we would carry a used auto tire and then roll it down the full flight of stairs toward passing cars. Upon doing so, we raced from her property, running in the opposite direction from the car (Jefferson Avenue was a one-way street) so that the irate driver couldn't apprehend us. Mind you, we never tried to hit the passing cars, but aimed our missile so that it would roll in front of the unsuspecting driver. We yelled with delight at the shock on the drivers' faces as they hit the brakes to avoid a collision. Today, I shudder at what could have gone wrong with such a prank but back then, to a group of nine- to ten-year-olds, it was great fun.

The third brownstone housed the Fee family: Phil Fee the father, Nan the mother, daughters Rosemary and Peggy, and sons Francis and Johnny. Francis suffered from cerebral palsy. He and I could and did communicate with each other, but only in a limited way since he was difficult to understand and confined to a wheelchair. I remember little of Johnny since he was considerably younger than I. Rosemary and Peggy played with my sisters, though Rosemary and my sister Helen both loved and hated each other. There were frequent battles between them and ever-recurring truces and make-ups. The Fees became close friends of my family and, like the Behans, helped us enormously after my father died with friendship, advice, and genuine sociability. We referred to Mr. Fee as the "big, bad wolf" since he enjoyed scaring us with his feigned wolf-like growl as he chased us through their home. Today I credit him with my lifelong academic endeavors since he got me into elementary school a year before I would have been eligible.

Apparently, as a young lad, age five, I tried everyone's patience with my childhood antics and ferret-like energy. As a last resort, friends of my mother suggested that she try to get me into the first grade at the local parochial school, Our Lady of Good Counsel (in those days, that school had no kindergarten). A widow with three children under age five, she quickly acquiesced and off I went with her to meet the school's principal, Brother Martin, a Franciscan. Though sympathetic, he told her to wait another year since incoming students had to be six years old.

Crestfallen, we left the school, only to encounter Mr. Fee, the school's custodian, on the front steps. My mom told him about my rejection. He exclaimed, "We'll see about that," and marched us back to Brother Martin's office. In no uncertain terms he told the principal that he had to admit me since my mother needed some respite from my incessant antics and boundless energy. I presume today I'd be labeled hyperactive and incorrigible and diagnosed with Attention Deficit Disorder and it'd be said I was never destined to do anything meaningful in life. But back then I was merely considered energetic. Mr. Fee's argument worked. I started first grade at age five, the youngest in my class, and eventually the youngest in both my high school and college classes. To future students curious about my youth, I explained that I could only be labeled a child genius, a prodigy in their midst.

Of course, I always laughed and admitted that my being young and in class with them was due only to Phil Fee.

The last memorable family on this north side of Jefferson Avenue lived near the corner, close to Howard Avenue. I'll call them the Jacksons. Part Irish, part German, the Jacksons could only be described as bizarre, frightening, and dysfunctional. The parents enjoyed sitting on their front stoop, consuming large volumes of Rheingold beer, cursing and whacking whichever of their eleven children irritated them at the moment. Likewise, they argued and cursed at any adult passing by who looked askance at them. Most of their children behaved similarly, like chips off the old parental blocks, and because of their erratic and unpredictable behavior, my group steered clear of the Jackson boys. Some had the nasty habit of picking up dog manure in their hands and throwing it at us if we ticked them off. This loathsome act seemed to bother neither the parents nor the assailants. On one memorable encounter, one of the younger Jacksons actually put some of this offal in his mouth and spat at us! Even now I cringe at telling this. It goes without saying that all our gang avoided the Jackson territory, whenever we could, never venturing too close to their lair. Nowadays, I presume we could have the parents arrested for child neglect, inappropriate use of animals—or at least their manure—and a whole host of disreputable behaviors. Imagine the courtroom drama. Perhaps expert witnesses from People for the Ethical Treatment of Animals could testify for either the prosecution or the defense, and perhaps today the Jacksons might merit their own cable reality show, *The Jacksons of Jefferson Avenue*.

On that note we'll end our tour of the north side of Jefferson Avenue and cross over to the opposite side of the street.

The South Side of Jefferson Avenue

Crossing the street, we begin our travels up the other side of Jefferson Avenue, heading back towards Ralph Avenue.

Our first stop is the apartment where the first Puerto Rican family moved, probably around 1952. Here resided Ernie Melendez, who was my age. Ernie and his large family recently had immigrated from Puerto Rico, and at first we looked at him dubiously. As Peter Fiorillo reminded me, Ernie had a brother we called Mira, because every time Ernie would speak to him, he'd say, *"Mira, mira,"* which in Spanish means, "Look, look." Why he said this every time remains a mystery to me. (Ernie became an integral member of our street gang and was easily accepted by all of us after we gave up the fear of being hacked to death with a machete.)

A year later, another Puerto Rican family moved into an apartment on the next block, and one of their daughters—very attractive—would saunter down our street in a provocative fashion. We called her Mambo and whistled at her.

Our next stop finds the apartment building where Johnny McClorey lived. Johnny was my best friend (along with Peter Fiorillo) and simultaneously my arch nemesis. Johnny became the second kid I met on our block, introduced to me by his mom, a friend of my mom. We would often play together and frequently argue over the silliest of things, such as who would pick a game to play or who would play first base in a stickball game. But we always resolved the problem, and his parents were truly gracious and friendly. One summer evening, his dad invited a group of us to Ebbets Field to watch the Brooklyn Dodgers play the Pittsburgh Pirates. Ebbets Field mesmerized me. I'd never seen anything like its spectacular lighting and beautiful green playing field or the immense crowds cheering for the Dodgers and booing the Pirates, even to the point of threatening the umpires. What a welcome contrast to the drab concrete of Jefferson Avenue. This initial outing was followed by many more over the years, most of them financed by Borden's Ice Cream. Fans with ten ice cream sandwich wrappers received a free ticket to the bleachers, entitling them not only to the game but the pregame show sponsored by Happy Felton's Knot-Hole Gang. That deal introduced legions of Brooklyn kids to Dodger baseball.

Invited at the last moment to that first game, I rushed to get to Johnny's house and left my recently acquired secondhand bike in our front yard. After we returned from that memorable game, I found my bike gone. That stolen bike was my first encounter with crime, and it upset me to no end. I presume this experience constituted the origin of my interest in crime which blossomed into an eventual career as a sociologist/criminologist.

Continuing up the street, we come to the homes of Paddy Barrigan, Robbie Bogart, Vinny Sinerchia, and Arnold Lemaire, all to some extent core members of our "gang." Paddy claimed Spanish ancestry, emigrating from Spain's Canary Islands. His family actually had canaries as pets. Robbie "Bogey" Bogart was smaller and slightly younger than the rest of our gang and because of this was always assigned the onerous duty of halting car traffic at Ralph Avenue while the rest of us played stickball in the street. It's not as bad as it sounds since in the late '40s and early '50s few cars traveled the streets to hinder our play. The few parked cars actually helped our game, with their fenders serving either as first or third base, while the street's sewer covers served as home plate and second base. The farthest sewer was the home run boundary.

Vinny Sinerchia's brownstone front steps hosted a stoop on its second level which served as our board game play area. Each summer in late August we played Monopoly there. One classic game actually lasted three days. After most of us had gone bankrupt, Johnny McClorey and Joey "Butter Ball" Mazola dueled for two full days until finally "Butter Ball" emerged the winner. We all decided he'd end up a real estate tycoon somewhere out there, buying up foreclosed Park Places and Boardwalks across the nation.

Arnold Lemaire is but a faint memory since he was a latecomer to Jefferson Avenue, didn't attend Our Lady of Good Counsel with the rest of us, and moved only a few years later, probably to you know where. Quiet and shy, Arnold was part of us, but not central to our group. I do recall that my sister Helen and his sister Rosemary had been sent by Mrs. Lemaire to purchase a loaf of rye bread from Frederick's Bakery on Ralph Avenue. My sister told me that the two of them liked the loaf so much they ate half of it on the way to the Lemaire apartment. Mrs. Lemaire was upset and never sent them to the bakery again.

We next encounter Mr. Pat Duffy, a thin, wispy old man who had immigrated from Ireland eons before. He must have been at least eighty, and my sisters and I thought he had his eye on my widowed grandmother, then in her mid-seventies. She would have none of his romancing, however, calling him a "skittery bag" every time he came to our apartment under some obvious pretense. Granny always told him to go home to his wife. It didn't help that Duffy drove a horse and wagon, and collected all sorts of junk from the neighborhood — a truly disreputable occupation in Granny's eyes even though in the 1940s horses and wagons still abounded in our neighborhood with their owners collecting old clothes, selling watermelons and potatoes, providing services such as sharpening knives and scissors, and delivering ice to those apartments without refrigeration. Often we kids on the street would hitch a ride, hanging onto the back of a wagon, greatly disturbing the drivers. Frequently the drivers would use their whip to try to lash at us. I still sport a scar on my right thumb after having received the lash across my hand from the demon-driver of a watermelon wagon. That was the end of my "hitchy-on-a-wagon" career. It's probably the main reason I hate watermelons and wagons today, though nowadays wagon-drivers are in short supply. Come to think about it, I hated most fruits and vegetables long before my "whipping."

Horse-drawn wagons could be dangerous, but certain house stoops also could be somewhat precarious. As you may recall, Heinz the Nazi made us run to avoid his chewing tobacco spittle. You heard the shout "Incoming!" from friends who saw him preparing to spew his wad or, even worse, readying his can of ready-made "juice" to dump on unsuspecting victims. Well, the south side of the street also had its own similar villain, nicknamed "Niagara." This middle-aged deranged woman occupied the second-story apartment directly across from my house. Since we frequently played stickball in the street, her stoop served as an ideal dugout for those awaiting their turn at bat. She didn't take kindly to our sitting there. To dissuade us she carefully opened her window and attempted to pour a bucket of water on us. When anyone heard the window opening, he'd yell "Niagara!" and everyone would quickly run from the stoop-dugout. However much she tried, she never actually hit anyone, but she sure soaked and ruined our seating area for the game's duration.

The Mazolas' apartment came next. Their son "Butter Ball" Joey (so named not because he was fat, but because his muscular body was rotund) actually ran our "gang" until he, too, left for suburbia. Big, friendly, self-assured, and two years older than the rest of us, he organized our play and our escapades. He also was the best fighter in our group. His father owned a roofing business, and I can still see in my mind his truck parked across from my house.

In the same building where Butter Ball lived, Louie Mione resided with his parents and his sister Josephine in the first-floor apartment. Louie was not only the best athlete on the street but also the best looking of all of our group. An Adonis in our midst! Adept at stickball and basketball, he outshone the rest of us. Years later, Louie and I attended St. Francis College together.

As we near the terminus of our Jefferson Avenue tour, we come to two apartments remembered for the tragedies that befell the occupants of both. In the first apartment lived a single Irish "business woman," approximately sixty years old. I knew nothing about her except that she always dressed immaculately and went to "business" daily. She attempted suicide on a number of occasions, each time the same way. Before going to sleep in the early evening, she would turn on the gas heating unit in her room but always leave her front apartment door slightly ajar. Predictably, the second-floor tenant would come home from his job punctually at the same time each day, smell the gas, run into her apartment, open the windows, shut off the gas, and call the police. This occurred numerous times until one fateful day when the upstairs tenant was delayed at work. He missed his usual rendezvous and the business woman died of gas inhalation. Most of the block remained convinced that she didn't truly wish to kill herself, and that her episodes constituted actual calls for help.

The second sad event, which is seared in my brain, took place in the apartment of an elderly recluse near the corner of Ralph Avenue. No one really knew much about her. She always dressed in black, reminding our group of the Wicked Witch in *The Wizard of Oz*, for whom she could easily pass. She seemed to have no family or friends. Never friendly, she clearly voiced her irritation with the antics of all the kids on the street. One day, in the heat of a July scorcher, police and firemen were called to her building. They immediately exited to put on gas masks and return to her apartment. Apparently she had died a few days earlier, unnoticed by others in the building until the odors of body decay attracted their attention. Most of the block assembled to watch the visibly upset police and firemen coming and going into and out of the building. Eventually Father Francis McCabe arrived from our church, Our Lady of Good Counsel, donned a gas mask, and gave her the Last Rites. He emerged clearly shaken and nauseated by what he had witnessed. I often wonder what kind of life she led and still feel somewhat ashamed over our disdain and mockery of this poor old woman, ignored by all except for her tragic end wherein she became the talk of the neighborhood. To be remembered only because of her death is truly a sad end to a life lived in a minor key.

As we near the end our virtual tour of Jefferson Avenue, we next encounter the building inhabited by Uncle Fred, one of the most colorful and controversial characters on the block. Uncle Fred appeared on our street every June, just as schools closed for the summer vacation. From the gossip on the street, we believed he lived in Florida and would spend his summers in Brooklyn, residing with his sister in the large apartment building near Ralph Avenue. Tall, balding, wiry, about sixty years old, the image of New York's former mayor Ed Koch, Uncle Fred quickly met all the boys on the block and made friends with us. He organized weekly tours and excursions to all sorts of interesting places such as Prospect Park, Coney Island, Brighton Beach, and the caves in Inwood Park in northern Manhattan. For some unknown reason, none of the moms on the street objected to his leading eight to ten of us on these trips. I guess they knew his very likable sister and consequently trusted Uncle Fred. He reminded us of a Boy Scout leader, without the title.

But in a certain sense, Uncle Fred came across as a modern day version of *Oliver Twist's* Fagin since he often scammed his way through these trips. On a typical excursion, he would tell all the boys on Jefferson Avenue to assemble in front of Peter Fiorillo's apartment house at 10 am. From there we would set off for a day at the beach, generally to Coney Island. Quite averse to any of us paying the fare on the BMT Jamaica Line subway, he instructed us to do one of two things. If he could engage the

transit ticket agent in conversation, we were supposed to crawl on all fours under the agent's booth,
continue under the turnstile, and then run up the
stairs and board the train just pulling into the station. But if the ticket agent refused to socialize,
Uncle Fred put his second scheme into play. It was
far less sophisticated. He told us to await the approach of the elevated subway train, which we
could see and hear coming from the previous Gates
Avenue station, and then, as a group, we were to
run up the stairs, jump the turnstiles, and board the
train before transit police could be summoned.
During these pseudo-criminal escapades, Uncle
Fred would feign shock over our antics, complaining loudly to the ticket agent about the incorrigible
delinquents who engaged in such morally repre-
hensible behavior. Fortunately, the transit cops
never apprehended us. In this neighborhood, we
were the least of their problems.

Arriving at Coney Island, Uncle Fred would
march us to Ravenhall Swimming Pool and pro-
ceed to get us in there free of charge as well. He
would tell the cashier that our group were orphans
from the St. John's Catholic Orphanage in Rock-
away, Queens, too poor to pay the admission price.
Often challenged because he had a very pro-
nounced Brooklyn Jewish accent, the cashier would
ask, "How come you, a Jew, are in charge of Catholic boys?" Uncle Fred didn't bat an eyelash. "I volunteer at the orphanage and am studying to be a

Catholic and my assignment is to assist these poor waifs who need a day at the pool and the beach. Won't you help them by giving them a day in the sun, relieving them of the daily misery of their orphanage?" It never failed, and we never paid the admission price there or anywhere else we traveled with our mentor, including riding on the world famous Wonder Wheel at Coney Island.

A few things did make us curious about Uncle Fred. First, he always held our money, claiming that it would be safer with him rather than having us lose it in the locker room or in the sand. None of our group claimed to be arithmetic geniuses, but we did notice that when he returned our money, we were always short a few nickels or dimes, which in those days constituted quite a bit. We usually set our suspicions aside and simply chalked the loss up to our failed monetary memories of how much money we started with. Second, and very strange to us, he liked to dry some of the boys with their towels after they exited either the pool or the ocean, hugging them as he did so, an honor extended only to a few chosen boys in our group. I often wondered why I was not so honored. I also wondered why he would demand that some of these same kids kiss him. Mind you, he did this in broad daylight in front of everyone and never really caused any great concern or upset in any of us until Tommy Scott (who lived on the next stretch of Jefferson Avenue) spilled the beans. Tommy had learned the facts of life before any of us, and he was the one who surmised that Uncle Fred was a lecherous, perverted pedophile, to be shunned at all costs. We naively had no idea what this meant, but as word spread throughout the block, Uncle Fred quickly became a pariah and soon disappeared forever, presumably back to Florida. In spite of Tommy's allegations, I can say that none of our gang appeared traumatized by Uncle Fred, and in fact, we all had a good laugh about his behavior. Most of our gang maintained a grudging admiration for him and for all the wonderful adventures and excursions he conducted over three successive summers. We did feel sorry that his sister had to live with such a despicable person, and although no one held it against her, I must admit that I still wonder how many nickels and dimes Uncle Fred gypped me out of.

On both sides of Jefferson Avenue lived older boys. We referred to them as the Big Guys—Junior Alcott, Joey Platz, Gus Dennis, among others. Some were quite tough. One of them, upon meeting Peter Fiorillo a few years ago, asked, "Did I ever beat you up?" In many ways, they became, for better or worse, role models. I recall sitting on the curb of the street admiring how they smoked, played stickball, and harassed teens from other streets.

I should say a word or two about the neighboring bordering avenues—Ralph Avenue and Howard Avenue—that enclosed Jefferson and more or less comprised the geographical limits of my early life. Both streets expanded the list of characters found on Jefferson. Sadie's Candy Store on Ralph Avenue housed the place where all of the kids on the block bought candy, daily newspapers and bottles of soda. Sadie and her husband Sam ran the business. Both hated doing their own laundry, so Sadie hired Peter Fiorillo and me to carry their dirty, smelly laundry to the laundromat one block away and do their wash. We were paid ten cents each per week for our services. We both hated the job, but feared that if we refused, we could never shop in Sadie's again. The only nice part of the task was that in the winter we could stand outside the laundromat under the exhaust vent and bask in the moist hot air—as long as we didn't mind being covered with lint.

Across the street from Sadie's, August Arndt's German delicatessen provided the neighborhood with excellent cold cuts. But the store had an inglorious past. Its previous owner, a German, probably a Nazi spy, had been arrested by the FBI during World War II. My mom told us that a few years earlier the Feds arrived and took the spy out in handcuffs. Apparently he had a shortwave radio concealed in the back of the store and was communicating with the Nazis. Since our neighborhood didn't comprise the center of the American war effort, everyone wondered what possible information he'd been sending to Berlin. Or perhaps Jefferson Avenue was the center and the spy was in cahoots with Mr. Heinz, the Nazi matron, and Sister Nazi.

A few other businesses appear in my mind's eye. Foremost among these is Frederick's Bakery where all the kids of Jefferson would go to retrieve the crusts of bread from the store's bread slicing machine. For free! Across from Frederick's, you would find Wolf's Grocery store which my family rarely used because my mom thought Wolf charged too much. The only day the entire block shopped there was the day Mr. Wolf hosted a star pitcher from the Brooklyn Dodgers, Joe Black, who purchased something from the store. Joe, a right-hander, won the first game in the 1952 World Series (Dodgers vs. Yankees), was the first black pitcher to win a World Series game, and earned the Rookie of the Year honor in 1952. I never did get inside the store that day, but I remember the large crowd milling around the entrance hoping for Joe's autograph.

On Howard Avenue, the Bushwick Hospital dominated most of the block, but most of Jefferson Avenue chose to take our medical chances at King's County Hospital in the East Flatbush section, quite a distance from our neighborhood.

Sal's Barber Shop could be found on Howard Avenue across from the Bushwick Hospital. Sal, the barber, constantly chattered with all his customers and even to this day Peter Fiorillo praises his barber qualities. But I never liked Sal. This dates to the time he made noises around my ears with his scissors, claiming he was giving me a haircut. I was about eight years old at the time, and when I arrived home my mom wanted to know why I didn't get my hair cut. I told her I did! She took me, along with Mrs. Fee, back to Sal's and read him the riot act. I eventually got an excellent haircut, but I feared going back there ever since. He might have scalped me.

I should tell you that some of the mothers were very assertive. Victor Herbert recalled that one of the boys, either Eddie or Vinny, who lived around the corner from me, liked to ride his bike, and was told by his mom never to ride it in the street. The one time he did he got hit by a car. As he lay there in the street, his mother, hysterical, came up to him, started smacking him and screaming at him, "How many times did I tell you not to go in the street?" Fortunately, he was not hurt badly.

And so our virtual Jefferson Avenue tour comes to its conclusion, leaving behind its curious characters and interesting situations. Undoubtedly the neighboring streets—Putnam Avenue, Madison Street, Hancock Street and Halsey Street—could boast or bemoan similar situations and memorable characters. Yet with the passage of time to those of us living in today's somewhat colorless suburbia, these memories take on an almost mythological quality and assume a much greater nostalgic importance than when they actually occurred. Today Jefferson Avenue looks far smaller than I remember it and the street life of yesteryear is long since gone, replaced with new residents, new situations, and new anecdotes.

Going to the Monroe

When my friends and I ventured away from our street, we went to the local movie houses, four of which were within four blocks of Jefferson Avenue. These were the RKO Bushwick, the elegant Lowes Gates, the Empire, and the best of all for kids, the Monroe. The Monroe was truly the pits, but every kid in the neighborhood loved it. Going to the movies was the focal entertainment point of our week, and the kids on Jefferson Avenue "lived" in the movies, going to them virtually every weekend when school was in session and several times a week during summer vacation.

Let me describe for you what it was like back then in what's now considered the Golden Age of cinema. But first you have to understand that we kids had "seasons" for everything we did.

These seasons structured our street lives, since most of our time revolved around block activities. We lived in the street; home was merely where we ate and slept and took a bath every Saturday night whether we needed it or not. As another friend, Sean Fanelli, reminded me, our lives revolved around our seasons and our four sewers on Jefferson Avenue: home plate and second base for stickball; two sewers for the goal posts in touch football and roller skating hockey; and four sewers for an automatic home run in stickball, which no one ever achieved, though we thought Louie Mione might have done so.

I still wonder who determined the dates and sequences of our annual rituals. These seasons had the same precision as the Vernal Equinox or Summer Solstice. By the middle of 1951, we'd already completed our swimming junkets to the indoor pool at the Hotel St. George in downtown Brooklyn (always followed by a visit to the local Horn and Hardart automat where we devoured the baked beans and chocolate pudding); the burning of the discarded Christmas tree season (January 1-20); the belly whopping sleigh season (January 21-31); the ice-ball war season (February 1-28); the rubber band-paper clip war season (March 1-20); the Jumbola marble season (March 21 to April 1); the small marble season (April 2-9); the Ringolevio season (April 10-20); the linoleum carpet gun season (April 21 - May 2); the burning of model airplanes season (May 3); the burning of Hitler's and Mussolini's cardboard houses season (May 4); the burning of sidewalk ants season (May 5); and the stickball season (May 6 - August 20).

Still to come were the sand pyramid building at Coney Island season (August 21-25); the roller skate season (August 26 - September 1); the Chinese handball season (September 2-9); the bottle top collecting season (September 10-14); the Johnny-on-a-pony season (September 15-21); the stoop ball season (September 22 - October 20); the Chinese checkers season (October 21 - November 1); the comic book trading season (November 2 - December 1); and, finishing the year, the visiting Santa season, assuming Santa risked returning to the local Woolworth's. We tried to keep the seasons from overlapping, but if they did, we didn't mind too much since our primary recreation was going to the movies year round.

By July 1, 1951 we were smack in the middle of our summer movie season (June 18 - August 31). On that day in July, the Monroe was showing the film every kid on Jefferson had eagerly awaited, *Abbott and Costello Meet Frankenstein* in which Wolfman meets his end falling off a cliff as he grasps the wings of Dracula.

The Monroe was the kind of movie "dive" you just don't see these days. Even in the 1940s and 1950s it was an oddity, but at least it was local and cheap. On Tuesdays and Wednesdays in the summer, the admission price was 11 cents, which entitled you to one Movietone newsreel complete with pictures of earthquakes in Turkey, floods in the Midwest, and President Truman's daughter Margaret playing the piano; five Sylvester and Tweety Bird-type cartoons; four coming attractions (now called trailers), repeated twice in the course of the afternoon (in case you missed the first showing while buying candy); one half-hour cowboy serial of the Tom Mix-Hopalong Cassidy-Lash LaRue genre; one Positively-No-Smoking-in-the-Orchestra sequence, sponsored by the city's fire department; and finally two full-length features. The first was generally dreadful since it was usually a romantic melodrama which nauseated the assembled kids, but the second often was an excellent classic such as *Four Feathers* (I still recall Lt. Harry Faversham with the branded scar of the Sengali tribe on his forehead) or *Angels with Dirty Faces* (did Rocky Sullivan really turn yellow when he went to the electric chair?). In addition, you received a free comic book (if you were under twelve) or a free dinner plate, cup, or saucer (if you were female and over twelve). The comic books never survived the afternoon since they were read in the dark during the romantic movie. The dinner plates generally did survive but were immediately consigned to collecting water under mother's flower pot. That was the Tuesday-Wednesday fare. On Saturdays, a similar program was presented, minus the comic book and dish, at the outrageous weekend price of 18 cents.

On certain Saturdays, no feature films were shown. The program consisted of *21 Cartoons*. Yet the management chintzed even in this because they never showed twenty-one of them. Peter Fiorillo, who served as our scribe, counted no more than sixteen on a given Saturday. Since the rest of our mob couldn't concentrate long enough to tally all of them, we rarely knew the difference. I suspect Peter demanded a portion of his eleven cents admission in return for this false advertising, but he probably got nowhere with his request.

The Monroe had other features of significance. For example, you always sat with your feet tucked under you because the floor beneath the seats oozed a mucky permafrost substance comprised of dried Kool-Aid, Pepsi-Cola, rancid peanut butter, discarded popcorn, foul-smelling remnants of un-digested Goobers and Raisinettes, and an assort-ment of small, crawling creatures which thrived in darkness. To reach the aisle, you walked on the other seats rather than step in the quicksand below. The bathrooms were even worse and one never used them except in the most dire emergencies. All the mothers on Jefferson Avenue had forbidden us to go anywhere near these "rest rooms." To get permission to go to the Monroe was difficult enough, but you could generally swing it if you promised Mom you'd use your own bathroom before going out.

Once we got our mothers' permission, we still had to get to the Monroe, which was no easy matter, even though it was only three blocks away. To reach the theater, our gang of boys from Jefferson Avenue had to cross hostile territory, which included such landmarks as the gypsy tattoo parlor on Howard Avenue. Since all of us knew that gypsies ate babies and sometimes young kids, we would race past their store to avoid their infamous "evil eye" which could hypnotize you, rendering you immobile and paralyzed. To the best of my recollection, everyone always made it.

The second and more hazardous obstacle was getting past the Madison Street boys who would become, a decade later, members of one of the most violent and feared street gangs in Brooklyn, the El Quintos. In our era the Madison Street kids merely robbed us, but only if there were more of them than us. We weren't mugged in today's barbaric way, either. Then the theft was done with finesse and hustle. Their leader would ask to borrow some money. I would answer, in ritual fashion: "I don't got no money." He would then ask to search me. I would consent (or else be jumped by his entire group). If money were found, the thieves would "borrow" it, to be paid back in the year 2020. Who knows? In a few years I might recoup my "investment" plus interest. If no money were found on any of us, we went on our way, no questions asked.

Of course, we Jefferson Avenue kids perfected ways of concealing our money. All money on Jefferson Avenue was controlled by the mothers. When they gave us some we sat down, took off our sneakers, and concealed it inside our socks. On days when we were going to the Monroe, we made sure our socks had been on our feet for at least four previous days. The smellier the better; after all, even if the Madison Street kids knew the money festered in our stinking sneakers, would they risk handling it? And so we would make it safely to the Monroe, where we would then sit on the curb and remove our concealed money to the bewilderment of all adult onlookers—except for the cashier, who was quite familiar with our ritual. Ah, the poor woman. Rumor had it that she eventually had been shipped to a lepers' colony somewhere in the South Pacific!

The program at the Monroe, which always started at 11:50 a.m. and ended precisely at 5:40, took the entire afternoon. But if you happened to be first in the waiting line, you were out of luck. The matron in charge of seating put you in the last row of the Children's Section. In those days, movie houses employed matrons and ushers who dictated where you sat in the theater. Rumor had it that this matron was also an ex-Nazi, rejected by the Gestapo because of her cruelty. When she was out of earshot, we would sing, "Hotsy, totsy, another little Nazi, hotsy, totsy, another dead Nazi." To this day whenever I see History Channel videos of the Gestapo, I instinctively think of that Monroe matron. Those who came to the Monroe later sat in progressively better rows closer to the screen. To add to the irony, you couldn't change your seat for fear of risking the permafrost ooze on the floor and the wrath of the Nazi matron. Not even tough, streetwise kids from Brooklyn would be so fearless.

Then there was the theater manager who, by some strange quirk of my memory, bore an amazing likeness to the Wizard of Oz. This nameless owner was somewhat aloof and rather dignified because of his pure white mane. Occasionally, though, his anger would explode, particularly when the jeers coming from the assembled kids during the highpoint of the romance film reached riot proportions or when the film projector broke as it inevitably did. He would then ascend the stage, turn on the house lights and announce that if peace were not immediately restored, the movie wouldn't continue. As soon as he finished his announcement, the rabble would yell, curse and scream, and throw paper cups, orange peels, and half-eaten Devil Dogs. At that point the manager would rapidly exit and the film would resume.

Just after 5 p.m., the final phase of Monroe life took place. This was the inevitable arrival of the anxious mothers who barged into the theater looking for their kids who had faithfully promised to be home by 5 for supper. But finding the right child was virtually impossible since the best part of the feature film was usually in progress at that time. It was always after 5 that Gunga Din was preparing to climb the golden turret. At such crucial moments, one could hear voices whispering frantically in the darkness: "Solly, are you in there?" "Joey, get out here this minute." "Jamesie, duck, here comes your mother." If you were unfortunate enough to be spotted by your mother, you would bargain for a few extra minutes of viewing time, generally with the suggestion that your mother might like to see the terrific ending.

One Saturday in July of 1951, all the Jefferson Avenue kids were ready for the trip to the Monroe. To our bitter disbelief, though, the mothers on the block apparently had consulted each other and decreed that none of us would be going to the Monroe that day. (As I mentioned, all decisions were made by the mothers on Jefferson Avenue.)

Vinny, Bop, Johnny, Louie, Peter, Wilbur, Joey, Bogey, Paddy, and I bemoaned our sad fate while sitting on Vinny's brownstone stoop. For a bunch of ten-year-olds, being barred from the Monroe was a cruel blow. But we were not despondent for

Collection of Peter Fiorillo

Peter Fiorillo, Billy Ritchie, and me.

long; both rebellion and leadership suddenly emerged in the person of Johnny McClorey.

Johnny stood up and announced, "I've had it! That's no way to treat a bunch of kids!" To his amazed disciples, he uncovered his plan to secure maternal permission for our Saturday venture. Quickly, the plan was put into action. We gathered all of the other kids on the block (only boys were considered kids) and Johnny arranged us, single file, at the corner of Ralph and Jefferson avenues. Your place in line was determined by how well you could count. The kids who could count to fifty were at the head of the column. I was near the end. McClorey then marched us to the first house, Peter Fiorillo's.

At the signal, the first on line rang the bell. Peter's mother answered (all door bells were answered by the mothers on Jefferson Avenue) and the kid asked, "Peter Fiorillo's mother, can Peter Fiorillo go to the Monroe?" "No." The door slammed. That kid would then leave and give a signal to the second kid on the line who would count to fifty, ascend the stairs, and ring the bell again. "Peter Fiorillo's mother, can Peter go to the Monroe?" "No." The door slammed again. The second kid would leave and the third kid would repeat the procedure. Predictably, after the ninth or tenth attack wave, Peter's mother had been worn down by group pressure and gave Peter permission to go to the Monroe.

Flushed with victory, Johnny marched his rabble to the home of the next victim, Bop's mother. This time Johnny needed only six lieutenants because Bop's mother caved in quickly once she heard that Peter's mother had given him permission. Domino style, each of the reluctant mothers capitulated when she was told, "Peter's mother, Bop's mother, and Jamesie's mother said they can go. Why can't I?"

The assault took less than an hour. By 11:45 all the kids had permission. We had our eighteen cents admission, plus five cents for the soda machine. We had our brown paper bag which contained a peanut butter sandwich, a never-to-be-used napkin, and a banana. Finally, we all had the same orders, "Be home at 5 o'clock and don't go near those filthy bathrooms." Off we went to confront the Howard Avenue gypsies, the Madison Street Boys, and the unknown perils of the greatest theater in Brooklyn.

A Cat Named Hitler

Let me digress a bit from the geography and characters of Jefferson Avenue, from the movie-going experience, to tell you about the only pet I ever had—a cat we called Hitler. Cats, dogs, and other small birds and animals abounded everywhere on Jefferson Avenue, many running wild but most kept in the apartments of many of the streets' residents, who lavished enormous love and affection on their beloved critters.

Paddy Barrigan's family hosted a number of singing canaries that entertained visitors with their melodious, lyrical sounds. Since Paddy and his family immigrated from the Canary Islands, word on the street said that they brought the birds with them. Maybe they'd been concealed in ventilated suitcases. How Paddy ended up with a seemingly Irish name remains a mystery. Perhaps it had something to do with the sinking of the Spanish Armada off the west coast of Ireland more than 400 years ago.

Next door to Paddy, Johnny McClorey's family had a dog named Spud. Spud was actually part Spitz, part Chow, but he must have considered himself part wolf since he readily attacked anyone incurring either his or Johnny's disfavor. I held the block record for the most Spud bites, four, though I actually came to like this four-legged assassin in his occasional non-lethal moments.

Teeming numbers of mice, rats, and stray cats populated the cellars of the street's apartment buildings, obviously unclaimed by any of the residents. They were the truly homeless of Jefferson Avenue, the denizens of the street's underworld. We heard that other households on the street actually possessed snakes and exotic reptiles, though this could never be confirmed.

My youngest sister Bunny had a fondness for cats. She and her friend Barbara McCaffery would often visit an elderly reclusive lady who lived in a large home on Bushwick Avenue, with her cats — almost fifty in total. Bunny and Barbara would remark how some of these cats would wrestle with each other, entertaining the two unsuspecting girls.

Weeks later, kittens would appear out of nowhere! Sometime later Bunny rescued one such homeless stray cat from the veritable zoo underneath our Jefferson Avenue houses. Even today, she claims it followed her to our second-floor apartment where she gave it a generous saucer of warm milk. It worked. The cat fell for the bait and devoured the milk in record time. Although Mammy wanted no part of having this "wild" cat as a pet, she consented to the animal staying just for the night because of my sister's pathetic tears and pleas. "It's out of here in the morning!" she exclaimed. But we knew that she secretly loved animals and actually felt sorry for this poor stray, so we weren't surprised that the cat still lived with us two years later.

For a long time, this black-and-white male cat remained nameless. We simply called him "Cat," "Kitty," or "Kitty Cat." This abruptly changed after my mom's close friend Mildred visited us. Seeing the animal for the first time, she remarked that Kitty had a black moustache that reminded her of the one Hitler had possessed. She thought it would be nice to call the cat "Hitler"! "Yes, it would be a good idea to name him Hitler since he looks so much like him," Mildred said. Believe it or not, as I write this, there is a website called www.catsthatlooklikeHitler.com . My cat was fifty years ahead of its time!

Lacking Mildred's imagination, I saw no such resemblance to the recently departed dictator. To me this cat looked like any ordinary black-and white stray which just happened to have a bit of black fur under his nose. How Mildred envisioned the Führer's countenance baffled me. For that matter, she could have named him "Stalin" or "Charlie Chaplin" or even "Thomas Dewey." Ah, but I realized that Mildred often had some strange ideas and notions when it came to animals. She had a parrot that could speak no English! Imagine that—a parrot that had never been taught, "Polly want a cracker" or other universal parrot-talk expressions.

Calling our cat Hitler appalled me. My anxiety about the cat's name related to the fact that many of the Jefferson Avenue residents were German, Jewish, or Italian, with fresh, vivid memories of the atrocities of the war which only recently had ended. Yet the name Hitler stuck, for a number of the animal devotees on Jefferson Avenue remarked that the cat's face did indeed resemble a feline version of Hitler's face! Nevertheless, I continued to address him with the generic "Here, Kitty Cat" or "Nice Kitty" when we were on our own.

Bored perhaps with our apartment living, Hitler often sought to escape the contentment of domesticity by returning to the "wild." Attempts to lure him back home involved considerable effort on my part and assistance from my friends on the street. One such successful attempt has to be credited to Johnny McClorey, the unofficial leader of our gang at that time. (At this point Butter Ball had moved away; I wonder if he started the Mazola Margarine business. Perhaps he became the CEO of Butterball Turkey.) Johnny devised his plan, the African Safari Plan, which he borrowed from one of those Tarzan-like films which we ten-year-olds regularly viewed at the Monroe. Most such cinematic gems entailed African natives screaming, running, and beating their shields with spears as they encircled and trapped unfortunate frightened and terrorized lions and leopards. On this occasion, all our "gang" assembled for the big cat hunt—Johnny, our leader, along with Peter Fiorillo, Wilbur Taylor, Vinny Sinerchia, Paddy Barrigan, Pat Walsh, little Robbie "Bogey" Bogart, Louie Mione, Danny Feldman, Tommy Scott, Arnold Lemaire, and me. All were primed for the adventure.

McClorey divided the group in half; one half assembled at the east end of Jefferson Avenue, at Howard, the other half at the west end near Ralph. Lining abreast, the "hunters" marched down Jefferson Avenue beating on the garbage can lids they'd substituted for shields, converging slowly on the terrified cat, yelling "Here Hitler, Hitler, Hitler." Sure enough the natives flushed out our prey, trapping Hitler under a parked car near the middle of the street. But the cunning prey wouldn't exit its lair and any who tried to grab him were bitten and scratched. After a considerable period, the hunters became bored and left me alone with my spooked cat. Only after I had obtained a long string to which

I attached part of a hot dog did I entice Hitler from beneath the car into our front yard and back to our apartment. After several similar escapes and re-captures in the weeks that followed, our Hitler finally accepted domesticity, abandoning further attempts to return to the Jefferson Avenue wild. Like a wild stallion, Hitler the Cat, had been broken.

Now all of you pet lovers know that your be-loved animal possesses remarkable traits of intelli-gence, super-animal skills, and resourcefulness scarcely duplicated anywhere in the animal king-dom. But Hitler the Cat surpassed even the best and brightest of his time. Let me cite just one exam-ple of his stellar abilities.

Those of you accustomed to apartment living in the city know that cleaning up after one's cat "does its thing" is rather unpleasant. Ours was an era long before kitty litter hit the scene. Somehow this task became my responsibility, no doubt because I liked order and neatness (unlike my sisters). Prob-ably just to annoy me, the neatnik, Hitler used our family bathtub as his more-or-less favorite place to deposit his calling card. Even though it was rela-tively easy to clean up and wash down this daily mess, it irked me to do so. As a partial solution to my annoyance, I would wait till Hitler squatted in the initial stage of his "evacuation," and then quickly pick him up and hold him over the toilet bowl. This simplified enormously any clean up. Hitler's initial jump into the bathtub and his preparatory rituals of getting comfortable quickly alerted me to what he was up to. After numerous days of catching him in the act and holding him over the toilet, it became rather routine. I made sure I always rewarded Hitler after he had successfully accomplished his mission by petting him, saying, "Good job, Mein Führer." Positive reinforcement definitely enhances behavioral modification.

One day, to my surprise, Hitler ignored his usual routine. As I entered our bathroom, there was Hitler standing four-square on the toilet seat and "doing his thing!" I couldn't believe it. All I had to do was flush. Nowhere in the annals of feline science has such a stupendous feat ever been accomplished! This pattern continued day after day, and I made sure that I praised Hitler profusely and stroked him lovingly. I know that Hitler loved this, for under his infamous moustache I could clearly discern a feline smile.

Immensely proud of my housebreaking feat, I often invited my friends to witness this stupendous achievement. Johnny McClorey remarked that Hitler's intelligence might almost equal that of his dog Spud. Peter Fiorillo thought I should appear with the cat on the *Ted Mack Amateur Hour*. Vinny Sinerchia wondered if I could train Hitler to use toilet paper and even flush the toilet. I even thought of charging admission to view the kitty's exploit.

After this, Hitler became an integral member of our family. We even took him on picnics to Highland Park, about two miles from Jefferson Avenue. Unbeknownst to my mother, I would hide the cat in the bags and blankets which we carried to the picnics. Then, to my mother's chagrin, we would unveil Hitler who, thoroughly terrified, would run up the nearest tree. Now have you ever tried to get a cat out of a tree? Coaching a bear from its branches is far easier. I'd have to use the same trick as I did in the African Safari Ritual—a piece of meat tied to a string. After an hour or two Hitler would finally calm down, realize his hunger, and shimmy down the tree's trunk to indulge. After that, he would enjoy the rest of the picnic—like one of the family.

Hitler remained an important part of our family until 1951 when we moved to Halsey Street, three blocks away. Unfortunately, the new landlord didn't permit animals in his apartments, so we had to let Hitler return to the wild and become just one more homeless animal in the vast underworld beneath Jefferson Avenue. A sad time for all. But in the months to come, when I would return to Jefferson Avenue to play with my friends, I would occasionally come across Hitler, who seemed to be thriving. He would recognize me, let me pet him and, as only a true pet owner/lover would know, seemed to smile at me. If there is a Cat Heaven, Hitler (the cat, that is) is there, telling his fellow cats about his strange days on Jefferson Avenue and his very strange owner, who housetrained a cat.

Transitions

By the mid-1950s, Jefferson Avenue began to experience the phenomenal ethnic changes occurring in the Bedford-Stuyvesant section of Brooklyn. "White flight" of the Irish, Germans, Jews, and Italians became a near stampede, while incoming blacks and then Puerto Ricans moved into the void created by the departure of former residents.

Our family joined the exodus, yet we only moved three streets away, and not by choice. A couple from Jamaica purchased our building and made it patently clear that as new owners they wanted us and our upstairs neighbors, the Hills, out of the building. Since the apartments had been rent controlled, the only legal way to gain more rental income dictated that we and the Hills be "evicted" so that new higher paying tenants could take our places. The new landlord used all sorts of ways to force our move. The electricity and water were turned off at unpredictable times. The stairwell and hallways were "fumigated" with toxic insecticides, making it impossible to leave the apartments without a mask, or mouth/nose covering. Strangers brandishing knives silently stalked my mother as she entered or left the darkened vestibule of the building. The new owners heaped verbal abuse on the Hills, calling them "white Jewish trash" and us "white Irish trash." It worked. We got the message and found a new apartment at 709 Halsey Street, not quite the move to the lush country of Long Island but a distinct improvement over our menacing abode on Jefferson Avenue.

On the day of our move in the summer of 1951, my uncles unleashed their revenge on the new landlords, trashing our apartment, putting broken glass in the toilet, ripping out the linoleum, breaking the glass-encased French doors, and slashing the wallpaper. The landlord couple and their fellow renegades remained out of sight, all the better since my Irish uncles loved a fight and undoubtedly would have beaten them severely, so upset were they for the way my mother had been treated. But Mammy didn't want any trouble. Alas, I must admit that I relished every minute of this destruction, payback for the shabby treatment of our family and the Hills. Our black neighbors sympathized with us. They were appalled at the actions of their new Jamaican neighbor and helpless to do anything about the new landlord's tactics. They feared similar treatment from their landlords since they also occupied rent-controlled housing.

So with deep regret, we left Jefferson Avenue to move a few streets away. As far as I was concerned, though, we were moving to a foreign country. My sisters felt similarly bereft, convinced that we would never meet new friends on Halsey Street. Weeks earlier, anticipating the move, we actually purchased a game set called "52 Games" and reasoned that we would play one game a week in our new home and thus would have no need to meet new friends.

We never played any of the games. On the very day of the actual move we met the Halsey Street Monigles, an Irish family with numerous kids and cousins who quickly befriended us. What my sisters and I feared would be one of the saddest days of our lives became one of the happiest and we quickly fit well into the street life of Halsey Street, helped enormously by the Monigles who (thank God) owned the candy store near the corner of Ralph Avenue. There we could hang out, play, and, more importantly, meet all kinds of new friends.

Yet Halsey Street rapidly underwent the same demographic changes as did Jefferson Avenue. As the new lower-income minority groups moved in, tensions arose between the new and the old. The block self-divided into two camps. On our western end lived middle-class blacks, a few Irish, and even fewer nondescript whites; the eastern segment of the street housed largely lower-income blacks and one Irish family. These two camps barely coexisted and fights and arguments occurred frequently. Each group stayed on its respective part of the street, resentful of the other camp.

On one occasion, my eight year-old sister Helen had a fight with three black girls who scratched her face and beat her with her own jump rope. When my mother found out what had happened, she corralled the local police officer on the beat. He informed Mammy she would have to press charges against the three culprits, which she was reluctant to do. Instead she verbally blasted the three girls and told them to leave Helen alone.

The next day, the mothers of the three girls appeared outside our house and my mother engaged them in a truly horrific verbal screaming match from our apartment window, which no one but the Irish and blacks could hope to match. At the time our mom had just finished washing our living room floor on the building's third floor. The irate black women started climbing our brownstone's stoop leading to the second story, cursing and threatening violence to my mother as they climbed the steps! Mammy opened the window and poured the dirty contents of the floor wash bucket right on them! Furious and humiliated, they quickly retreated, cursing and threatening all sorts of violence as they went. But no one bothered my sister again. Hell hath no fury like a mother!

I spent little time on Halsey Street since I still often returned to Jefferson Avenue to play with my friends who still lived there. Yet one peculiar Halsey Street memory still remains. One cold, rainy Saturday morning I sat by my living room window, bored silly, just staring out at the street below. Suddenly, out of nowhere came a cat. In close pursuit there followed an enormous rat that caught the cat and killed it! I sat thinking, *Isn't it supposed to be the reverse? How could a rat bite the throat of a cat?* Is this what I actually saw or is my memory inventing this reality? If it did happen—I'm convinced it did—was it the first incident in all of human history where a rat killed a cat? I know my Jefferson Avenue cat Hitler would never have been attacked for he would have made short work of that Halsey Street rat.

The other indelible memory of our sojourn on Halsey Street relates to the growing problem of crime along the streets and throughout the larger neighborhood. Perhaps crime had always been a major concern of the area. Perhaps the early 1950s did register a quantum leap in criminal behavior relatively unknown in earlier decades. Perhaps it only came to my attention as I matured and became more conscious of the world and its problems. Regardless of the reasons, crime in general, and physical violence in particular, increasingly concerned everyone around us.

This concern struck home with my family when we heard about the murder of Otto, the local shoe repairman. Otto certainly wasn't liked by many of his neighbors and Mammy constantly warned my sisters to avoid his shop. His business occupied a small store on Ralph Avenue, around the corner from our Halsey Street apartment. Very dimly lit and sparse in its furnishings, it presented an ideal target for robbers and burglars even though the amount of cash on the premises had to be minimal. Otto also had a personality and bearing that could only be described as offensive, cantankerous, sullen, and somewhat nasty to his customers. Most locals resented him, and rumors abounded about his sexual advances, particularly toward teenage girls. My younger sister Bunny told me that Otto often asked her to kiss him when she picked up repaired shoes, but she would always run out of his shop before he came around the counter. How Mammy allowed her to go there alone puzzles me. Probably Bunny never told her about Otto.

But then one summer's day in 1952, we heard the news about Otto's murder. My sisters and I heard the rumor and quickly ran to his store outside of which a sizable crowd had assembled. In front of the cobbler's store entrance stood an enormous Irish cop from NYPD's 81st Precinct. He held a large nightstick and guarded the store as homicide detectives processed the crime scene. We begged the policeman to let us see the corpse. He looked down at us and said, "Now you wouldn't want to see a poor man like that lying dead on the floor in a pool of blood, would you?" YES, we would! After much pleading and badgering, we finally convinced him, and he allowed my sisters and me, along with dozens of local kids, to peer through the glass door. In the dim light I saw Otto's legs protruding beyond the countertop which concealed the rest of his body. We learned days later that he'd been stabbed multiple times by his assailant, a sixteen-year-old male intent on robbing the store. Our friends claimed they could see blood oozing near his legs, but I didn't.

Otto's murder highlighted the changing nature of crime in the area. With increasing regularity, robberies of pedestrians and businesses on Ralph Avenue, burglaries of apartments, sexual assaults on women, domestic violence episodes, and additional murders—most of which were teenage gang related—transformed my consciousness and the consciousnesses of everyone around us. By 1954, the area evidenced a neighborhood in the throes of a crime wave where you constantly "watched your back."

This fear extended to include the threat posed by the gangs that increasingly asserted their power in the area. Youth gangs had long been a presence in our neighborhood, but their activity had largely consigned itself into individual street membership and street "protection." Rarely had local gang activity spilled over into truly violent, homicidal activity. Earlier on Jefferson Avenue, all of the boys belonged to what outsiders would now consider a gang, though we never so identified ourselves and our criminal activity rarely moved beyond fist fights with each other. Yet protecting our Jefferson "turf" remained a tribal concern. Other boys from neighboring blocks clearly were unwelcome. On one occasion, a boy, approximately ten years old, rode his bike down our street. Since no one knew the interloper, the "gang" attacked him, probably at Butter Ball Mazola's direction. We destroyed his bike and chased him off the block. This incident served as a warning to other outsiders about our street's resolve to monitor and protect its boundaries. I had no doubt the same fate would have befallen me if I had ventured unescorted onto neighboring streets.

Another lasting memory of Butter Ball involves his encounter with a kid from a nearby street who came from an equally tough section of Brooklyn, the Gowanus neighborhood. When he moved in, this newcomer liked to boast how much better his old neighborhood was, how tough its kids were, and how far superior his old area was to everything in our neighborhood. Butter Ball got fed up with this bravado and organized all of us to jump the kid and rough him up, which we did, taking off his pants and throwing them up on the local street lamppost. In so doing, we discovered that he wore long underwear which we thought absolutely hilarious. We'd never heard of anyone sporting such attire. Defeated and humiliated, the victim ran off to his apartment, crying and shouting insults as he went. He emerged only weeks later, properly chagrined and humbled to the ways of our all-powerful Jefferson Avenue peer group, never again bragging about South Brooklyn. After this episode, he also became a core member of our gang.

Not only did our group discipline newcomers to the block, but we also whipped into shape those who tried to exert their selfishness over the rest of us. I remember one case in point. In winter, all of us would take turns on the only sled on the block to "belly whop" down the middle of snow-packed Jefferson Avenue. We would line up and patiently wait our turn on the sled, but Marco jumped the line, demanding to go ahead of the rest of us. No way would we permit him to do so. Angry and embittered, he left the group, returning a few minutes later with an ice breaker-type shovel. He proceeded to chop the ice upon which we sledded! We stared at him in disbelief for a moment before we jumped him. We beat him rather severely, breaking his shovel in the process. He ran, crying, back to his apartment. None of us saw him again till mid spring, at which time he resurfaced, much more willing to abide by our group's norms than he had a few months earlier. Again, the peer group exerted its will over deviant members.

Neighboring street kids also protected their turf from unwelcomed misfits. We'd heard that on Palmetto Street, a few blocks away, a Puerto Rican teen had robbed an elderly Italian woman, pushing her into her building's vestibule as she returned from grocery shopping. Quickly apprehended by the Italian teens who chased him onto the roof of an adjoining building, he somehow "flew" from the roof and died from his "fall." When police arrived, "no one knew for nothing."

On another occasion in our area, one of the Irish teens had been attacked and beaten by a group of black toughs who also stole his new jacket. Running home, he got his brothers, borrowed a neighbor's car, and cruised the area seeking his assailants. Eventually they spotted them running down the center of the street fleeing from the oncoming car. Gunning the motor, the driver literally ran over one of the culprits, retrieving the stolen jacket from the victim in the aftermath. When we inquired whether the black boy had survived, no one knew.

This Jefferson Avenue insularity diminished greatly as we became teens simply because we hung out more and more with friends from neighboring streets, mostly classmates from Our Lady of Good Counsel. Gradually our identification with the neighborhood extended to Putnam Avenue, Hancock Street, Madison Street, and Halsey Street. Our horizons had expanded!

But as our world expanded, so also did our encounters with the neighboring riffraff teens. One such unsavory character known as the Turk often bullied others, myself included. Over six feet tall and very heavy, he trapped me on Putnam Avenue and beat me, fortunately not very severely. Terrified of encountering him again, I avoided him where possible and worried what I would do if we inadvertently met each other again.

Well, I told two of my friends—Jimmy O'Boyle and Bruce Patton (not their real names)—what had happened. Jimmy and Bruce could only be described as "loose cannons," quick to fight and never willing to back down from unpleasant encounters. Their solution was simple; "Lets get the Turk and beat the $*@# out of him."

So they picked up their weapons, a garrison belt for Jimmy and a large motorcycle chain for Bruce, and the three of us set off to look for the Turk. About an hour later, we found him on Putnam Avenue where he had previously knocked me down and kicked me. Both Jimmy and Bruce threw the Turk against a wall and whacked his back and legs with the belt and chain. Bruce then grabbed him by his throat, yelling, "If you ever touch O'Kane again, we'll kill you!" The Turk, crying hysterically, pleaded for mercy. Whimpering in terror, he finally ran away. Jimmy watched him race off. "You'll never have a problem with him again," he told me, and I never did. In fact, the next few times I saw the Turk, he crossed the street to avoid me!

Victor Herbert, my fellow classmate, recently reminded me of Jimmy O'Boyle's often colorful behavior—most notably his Mother's Day escapades. Each year Jimmy would present his mom with a wonderful huge bouquet of flowers, beauties which any mother would cherish. Unbeknownst to his mother, Jimmy obtained his "gift" from nearby Evergreen Cemetery. Each year, on the morning of Mother's Day, Jimmy would ride his bike to the cemetery and gather flowers from the dozens of graves where they recently had been placed by grieving families. Mrs. O'Boyle, to my knowledge, never learned what Jimmy did. As one of Drew University's graduate students, Jaclyn Harte, remarked, "One person's graveyard flower is another person's beautiful centerpiece."

The Parish and the School

Before I become too involved in these street recollections, let me flash back to the parish church and the elementary school which I attended, since both encompassed so much of my early life. To locate it in physical space, let us again go back to our map (page 199). If you went to Ralph Avenue and turned right, and then turned left on Putnam Avenue, halfway down the street you would find Our Lady of Good Counsel, which comprised a beautiful Gothic church, two elementary schools (one for girls, one for boys), a large rectory which housed four or five priests, a convent with eight Sisters of St. Joseph nuns, a friary with at least six Franciscan Brothers, and finally a large communal hall where bingo, parish dances, and additional Sunday Masses were held. It was quite a complex at that time. Across the street from the two schools you would find Madison Street Park, which was all concrete. In the park, we would spend entire days playing basketball, stickball, and even football — yes, football on concrete — ouch!

In Brooklyn, in the 1940s and 1950s, the parish comprised the mainstay of not only the spiritual and educational life, but also the social life of those Catholics within its geographical boundaries. It was a veritable friendly ghetto which met just about every human spiritual and social need. In those times, you received your Baptism there and had administered to you the sacraments of Penance, Confirmation, and Holy Eucharist. You attended Mass every Sunday. You received your elementary education in the parish school and, in some adjoining parishes, your high school education. You were married there, and possibly even buried from there. To Irish Catholics, the parish offered a form of cradle-to-grave security since the world beyond consisted of a largely unknown area — a *terra incognita* — where you worked and earned a living. As an adult you could join the Knights of Columbus, the Holy Name Society, the Rosary Altar Society, or the St. Vincent de Paul

Society (which assisted poor families), all within the parish. You could play bingo, partake of an annual parish retreat (one for men, another for women), attend weekly Benediction services, or join in the annual Forty Hours Devotion held each February. As a male you could become an altar boy, join the choir, play on Catholic Youth Organization (CYO) basketball or baseball teams, join the parish Boy Scouts, or become a Columbian Squire, which was the junior branch of the Knights of Columbus.

These opportunities and activities describe not only Our Lady of Good Counsel, but just about every other parish in Brooklyn at that time. One could describe St. Thomas Aquinas in Flatbush, St. Michael's in East New York, St. Paul's in Gowanus, or Our Lady of Perpetual Help in Bay Ridge in the same manner. A homogeneity of parish life existed and Brooklyn Catholics understood this culture whether or not they chose to become involved in it. Then, you identified yourself mainly by your parish—"She's from Our Lady of Lourdes," or "He's from St. Rita's." Even our Jewish friends identified themselves by what parish they lived in. It's probably a stretch to say that most of our lives remained encapsulated within the confines of both the neighborhood and parish boundaries, but geography and religion came close to the self-identification of all those I knew and all of those with whom I rubbed elbows in that bygone era. In fact, I never really knew anyone other than Catholics or Jews until I attended graduate school at Columbia University. There I met and became a close friend of Don Schmid, a Protestant from North Dakota.

Yet all this has changed in the past fifty years. A recent visit to Our Lady of Good Counsel highlighted its demise. Both elementary schools have closed and the convent and friary no longer house any nuns or brothers. The church opens only for Sunday Mass since daily Mass is celebrated in the rectory, which houses only one priest, the pastor who so graciously spoke to me and conducted a brief tour of what's left. Crime has become an ongoing concern. The parish's former glorious structures are now ringed, sadly, with chain link fences complete with barbed wire. Hard times have radically altered Our Lady of Good Counsel, and the parish has merged with the adjoining one, St. John the Baptist, the final death knell to a once great institution.

So with much nostalgia, let me describe what it was like back then. By now you probably realize that I'm slightly inclined to romanticize and embellish my memories of this "ideal" past, but I doubt they are that far off from the reality of all those years ago.

I've already mentioned how I started my academic life through the "pull" of the "big bad wolf," Mr. Phil Fee, whose intervention allowed me to enter Our Lady of Good Counsel's first grade at age five. Let's look at the rest of my schooling there from 1946 to 1954 when I graduated from elementary school.

A brief word about the nomenclature of grades at Our Lady of Good Counsel might come in handy at this point. Because of birthday/age cutoff, you entered the first grade either in September (1A), or January (1B). Eight years later, the A sections graduated in June, the B section in late January. Occasionally very bright students skipped sections, for example, the 5A to the 5B, shortening their elementary schooling by six months. A true genius, Johnny McClorey, actually skipped a full grade. Alas, I never was so chosen, for reasons obvious to anyone who knows me.

My initial memories of first through fourth grades are cloudy, though recent conversations with Victor Herbert, a friend and fellow classmate whom I mentioned earlier, have filled in a few blank spaces in both our recollections. Our teachers were Miss Quigley (first grade), Miss Nichols (second grade), Miss Diamond (third grade), Miss Mitchell (fourth grade) and Miss Prince (who taught the second part of fourth grade, 4B). We called all the female teachers Miss, though I have no idea whether any of them had ever been married. I presume they were what we then called "spinsters"—women who had devoted their professional lives to attempting the education of Brooklyn's incorrigible youth. Two of these teachers do stand out in my mind: Miss Diamond and Miss Mitchell.

Miss Diamond clearly terrified me and, I suspect, most of my third-grade class. Middle-aged, short, wiry as a weasel and just as cunning, with a full head of hair arranged bouffant style, Miss Diamond always seemed to screech at us in a high-pitched, threatening voice. Perpetually in motion, she would berate anyone who did not perform to her standard. Occasionally she would clip you on the head with her emaciated rodent-like paw, signaling her disdain for your performance or lack thereof.

Once when I was in her third-grade class, I almost scalded myself to death with boiling water. For some unknown reason, Miss Diamond often utilized my services to carry a tea kettle of boiling water from the school's second floor to the teacher's room on the first floor. One morning, racing down the full flight of stairs, I tripped, spilling the kettle's contents on my legs. A big deal ensued; one of the school's mothers visiting the school raced to my house and shouted to my mom, "Tilly, get down to Good Counsel. James has been scalded!" It was all a tempest in a teapot (no pun intended) since I had not suffered any serious harm. Nevertheless my mother informed Miss Diamond what she thought of allowing a seven-year-old to transport boiling water anywhere, let alone down a huge flight of stairs. Ah, yes, the best part—I got the rest of the day off!

Somehow I survived third grade, relieved that I would be promoted to the fourth grade, finally rid of Miss Diamond. Yet early in that summer, rumors circulated that the principal would assign that same Miss Diamond to teach fourth grade come September. Horrors! My summer was totally ruined. Somehow my prison stay would be extended another year. Why do bad things happen to good kids? Something had to be done. But what could a soon-to-be eight-year-old boy do to avert another year's cruel fate? I did the only thing I could think of. I prayed to the Almighty that He strike me with polio so that I'd be excused from school in September. Mind you, polio had become almost epidemic then and I prayed only for a mild case, yet one serious enough to spare me another year with Miss Diamond. Crippled though I'd be, I'd at least be rid of the tyrant. Yet Fate and Heaven intervened since Miss Diamond stayed with the third grade.

In September, Miss Mitchell became our fourth grade teacher in 4A. The exact opposite of the tyrant, Miss Mitchell exuded warmth and friendliness, rarely if ever humiliating anyone in her charge. She was always kind and nurturing to the wild bunch under her care. Because of her, school became far less onerous for me, and I also thanked God for not striking me down with polio.

However, I do recall one truly scandalous event in Miss Mitchell's 4A class. While teaching us that homonyms sound alike but have different meanings, she cited a shocking example: "The boy walked down the street with a bare (bear) behind!" The class's shock and surprise eventually erupted in loud laughing and Miss Mitchell joined in the fun. We wondered whether she'd be fired if our new principal, Brother Angelus, ever found out. I now suspect he also would have enjoyed the play on words.

A word about the four consecutive Our Lady of Good Counsel principals: Brothers Martin, Bertrand, Angelus, and Stanislas. All were firm but fair disciplinarians whom we held in awe, fearing what they could do to us, yet respecting their professionalism in running a school with 500+ boys. In the first few grades, the teachers often warned us that if we misbehaved, we would be sent to the principal's office where there was a mechanical spanking machine which would mete out appropriate physical punishment. Believe me that kept us in line even though we knew no kid who had ever seen such a machine, let alone had been strapped into it. Yet none of us wanted to be the first to experience it. In reality, those kids who misbehaved indeed were sent to the principal, but suffered a far less serious punishment. They had to sit outside his office on a bench for a certain period of time, receiving only an oral reprimand for their disruptive behavior. I actually was sent to the principal's office only once, for talking in Miss Diamond's class. Obviously the punishment had no deterrent effect on my future and present loquaciousness. I am living proof of the uselessness of the threat of the notorious spanking machine, and the shaming of a few hours sitting on the principal's bench.

Our 4B teacher was Miss Prince, truly a wonderful, benevolent, kind-hearted woman whom all of us admired. My only memories of her relate to her kindness and softness, and all of the memories are pleasant. Nothing peculiar or eventful in either that 4A or 4B classes stands out in my mind. I guess there were no disasters to recount.

By contrast the fifth grade conjures many more memories—positive and negative—than previous grades. My 5A teacher, Brother John, remains my all-time favorite. He had never taught before his Our Lady of Good Counsel assignment. Older than the typical Franciscan, Brother John joined the order in his early thirties. Tall, quiet, and always polite, he won the admiration of our entire class, and his maturity stood in marked contrast to the much younger brothers who taught other grades. Some of the brothers were barely twenty-two years old, so Brother John's impact on my life remains a half-century later, primarily because he instilled a love of learning (even for a fifth grader) and opened up the "softer" side of the academic life at Our Lady of Good Counsel. You must remember that most Our Lady of Good Counsel kids came from difficult backgrounds where learning and intellectual curiosity comprised secondary qualities in our lives. Life on the streets took top priority.

My fondest memory of Brother John involves the field trip he conducted to the Museum of Natural History in Manhattan. One cold early December Saturday morning, he led us via subway to the museum, the first time any of the class had ventured beyond Brooklyn. We even stopped in a deli where he ordered hot soup for everyone, which we all greatly appreciated since the outside temperature hovered below freezing. The time spent in the museum flew by, all of us enraptured with the exhibits, particularly the African Plains, complete with the centerpiece of stuffed elephants and large dioramas displaying monkeys, lions, zebras, and leopards. Our field trip opened a brand new horizon to each of us, sequestered as we were in a fairly homogenous enclave in a small section of insular Brooklyn. Since then, I have taken many trips to that museum, remembering Brother John and his wonderful tour of that wonderful place. Over the decades, he and I kept up our relationship. He spent much of his professional career as the director of career development at St. Francis College in Brooklyn and died in 2006. To me, he will remain forever a great man who opened new vistas beyond my limited Brooklyn world.

I wish I could say the same of my next teacher. In the spring semester of 1951, 5B proved a startling contrast to 5A since our new teacher Brother Winston (not his real name, but he did look like Winston Churchill) could only be described as the exact opposite of Brother John. At least sixty years old, he was opinionated, nasty, vulgar in his demeanor, and quick to reprimand anyone who questioned his competence or leadership. He could only be described as a complete authoritarian with a sadistic streak that frightened us. Most of us feared him since he would physically discipline us if we crossed him. On one memorable occasion near the end of the term, he told the class to open the arithmetic text to page sixteen. We promptly did so. He then started asking questions which came from page seventeen. When we challenged him—sheepishly, of course—he denied he was at fault and screamed we were all wrong. In retribution he lined up the entire class and slapped each boy in the face. There were easily forty of us in his class. That semester ended none too soon, and my peers and I rejoiced when we were out of his clutches! The suspicion of lurid scandal always hung about Brother Winston, and, no surprise to any of us, he suddenly was transferred from Our Lady of Good Counsel after our term with him ended. I suspect Brother Stanislas, our new principal, saw the real Brother Winston.

Off to the sixth grade then, with Brother Gregory, a new, funny, quirky teacher. We believed him to be ancient, probably even seventy. He was short, a little stocky, with thick coke-bottle-lens glasses. Likable and humorous, he did his best to discipline the class, often to no avail. It's remarkable that we learned anything from him, but I guess we must have. Three clear memories of him lodge in my mind.

The first involved his attempt to discipline Frank Squidano. Frankie never paid any attention in class, rarely turned in his homework, and generally created chaos in the classroom. On one occasion, he dashed all around the classroom with Brother Gregory in hot pursuit, thrusting his wooden yardstick. Finally trapping him, Brother Gregory hit Frankie's wrist and watch and, to the amazement of all, the hands of the watch rapidly spun BACKWARDS. None of us had ever seen such an occurrence and all marveled at this new engineering phenomenon. Even Brother Gregory was amazed. He quickly forgot his disciplining escapade against Frankie and apologized for destroying Frank's Mickey Mouse watch.

Another memory survives completely intact of my time in 6A. In October 1951, a momentous sports event occurred, the final game of the three-game pennant playoff between the Brooklyn Dodgers and the New York Giants, the winner of which would make it to the World Series. For all of us sixth-graders, this was the game of the century. Brother Gregory had his radio tuned to the game, as did virtually everyone in Brooklyn and the Bronx. But school ended before the final inning and everyone raced home to be in on the climax. Virtually all of our class ran to Tommy Luhmann's apartment since he had one of the only TVs in the class, and he lived around the corner from Our Lady of Good Counsel. We piled into his dining room, sat on chairs, lay under the table, leaned against the wall, and watched the outcome. Then, at precisely 3:58 p.m. in the bottom of the ninth inning, with two men on base, Bobby Thomson of the Giants cranked a three-run home run off of Dodger pitcher Ralph Branca, winning the game and National League championship. The press called it the "shot heard 'round the world." We couldn't believe it! To this day, all Dodger fans, as well as anyone even vaguely conscious in 1951, can tell you where they were, what they did, and how they reacted to Thomson's stunner. It's like remembering Pearl Harbor, JFK and Martin Luther King's assassinations, and the terrorist attacks on 9/11 — something ingrained in a nation's psyche. Traumatized by the game's ending, all of us silently left Tommy's apartment, speaking to no one, bearing our shame and psychic trauma alone. Later came the only saving feature — the Giants lost to the equally hated Yankees in the World Series in six games!

The third vivid sixth-grade memory relates to Brother Gregory's daily afternoon nap in our class-room. Typically, he would return from lunch in the friary, start to feel sleepy around 1:30 p.m., tell the class to take out their texts and read pages such and such, and promptly fall sound asleep at his desk. Shortly before this ritual, he would send me to the parish auditorium to get a soda from the machine for him. I would do so around 1:35 p.m. and return with the soda only to find him sound asleep. I and the entire class kept very quiet, ignoring the text assignment, cavorting quietly with each other until 2:40 p.m. when on signal from my classmates, I would gently nudge him, offering him the soda. This left only ten minutes remaining in the class day at which time we were dismissed. He always seemed amazed that he had fallen asleep for most of the afternoon. This pattern continued for weeks, fueled by the warm days of spring wherein he slept ever so deeply. All in all, he was a good—not great—teacher, remembered kindly by most of us years later.

Brother Demas (not his real name) taught our seventh-grade class (7A and 7B). Young, hand-some, and volatile when provoked, he somehow managed more than forty boys, but did so by exact-ing fairly harsh discipline. His usual method con-sisted of a sharp slap to the face of any student who talked too much in class, who failed to turn in a homework assignment, or who challenged his authority. Ordinarily, this didn't upset any of us too much, since, you must remember, physical discipline constituted the norm sixty years ago. I frequently received a sharp slap for talking in class. When so disciplined, Brother Demas would call you to the front of the room, stand in front of you, and announce that if you moved your head or "flinched," you would receive a second slap. We took this punishment in a good-natured way, frequently saying, "I didn't flinch." He often responded, "Yes, you did." Even today I have no animosity toward his discipline, primarily because he was reasonably fair in its use.

This fairly benign pattern, however, changed dramatically when one of my classmates played hooky and returned the next day with an obviously forged note, allegedly from his mom, indicating that he had been sick and thus should be excused. Brother Demas immediately determined that the note was a fake and proceeded to exact what I and my fellow classmates considered cruel and sadistic retribution on the truant. Brother Demas literally paddled our classmate off and on for the entire morning! In between beatings, he verbally humiliated and mocked the victim. Finally, near noon, the boy ran crying hysterically from the classroom and subsequently was expelled from Our Lady of Good Counsel. My memory may be a little cloudy here, but I recall the boy's parents meeting the principal and appealing the dismissal to no avail. Subsequently, they appealed to Father Devanney, who was assistant pastor. He reinstated the student in the following eighth-grade term from which he did graduate with the rest of us in June 1954. Today, I can still vividly remember the sadism of Brother Demas and the total humiliation of my classmate.

Almost twenty years later, I accidentally met Brother Demas at a social function and mentioned that he had taught me in seventh grade. He avoided my glance, told me he had never taught me and in fact had never taught at Our Lady of Good Counsel! I persisted and he became somewhat combative, denying completely his involvement there, and quickly backed out of our conversation, completely stunning me with his refusal even to admit his full year at the school. After that, I learned from other Franciscan Brothers that he had left the order. I never found out if this was voluntary on his part or required by the Franciscan Order. Either way it was no loss for anyone in education.

Before we leave the seventh grade, I want to mention one other incident that sticks in my memory — the time a nineteen-year-old gypsy arrived in the class. It turns out that the local gypsies frequently approached the parish priests for financial handouts. After numerous "gifts" to the gypsies, one of the priests, Father Kelly, had had it. He told the gypsy parents he would give them no more cash since their children did not attend our school.

Lo and behold, the next day, a nineteen-year-old gypsy youth enrolled in Our Lady of Good Counsel and appeared in our class. Tall and heavy, he couldn't fit in the usual desk seat and had to sit in a regular chair near the door. He couldn't participate in any of the lessons, appeared ill at ease, and never answered any questions correctly. After lunch, he never returned and we learned later that Father Kelly gave his gypsy father some money, at which point the gypsy student and his clan disappeared. You have to hand it to them and admire the way they effectively worked the system.

At long last, the eighth grade and my final year at Our Lady of Good Counsel arrived. Similar to other grades, the eighth grade had two sections—8A taught by Brother Ralph and 8B taught by Brother Lawrence. Fortunately for all my fellow classmates, luck was with us. The scary time with Brothers Winston and Demas had faded into memory, and we thrived in the eighth grade. Now we were kings of the entire school, and we had two teachers whom we liked and even admired.

Brother Ralph, middle-aged, quiet, fair, and always firm but not excessively so, taught us a great deal, about math, history, and English, preparing us for our high school curricula, as did Brother Lawrence six months later. Brother Ralph convinced all of us that his real name was Archibald Benvenuto, which we believed. Only years later did I learn this was a fabrication.

Brother Lawrence, also middle-aged, could be quite tough if pushed, yet he rarely showed this trait, teaching us as a benevolent uncle might and rarely losing his temper. On one occasion, however, one of my classmates really provoked him, actually striking him, and then had the gall to challenge Brother Lawrence to a fist fight. Mind you, this fellow classmate was quite tough and we wondered what the outcome might be. He and Brother Lawrence stepped into the corridor. We listened in breathless silence. There came the sound of a fist against bone. In a few minutes, Brother Lawrence came in alone. Later our classmate returned sporting a large black eye. None of us witnessed the brief fight, but all saw the outcome. Most of us silently cheered our teacher, though we acted as if nothing had happened. But that ended all classroom threats.

Brother Lawrence's physical prowess also came in handy in the confrontation with the P.S. 26 kids who came to wipe us out one school day. Brother Lawrence and many of the other brothers could easily handle themselves in any physical fight and did so quite spectacularly in that confrontation. I suspect, as teenagers, they had been handy with their fists before their calling to the calmness of the religious life. In contrast to Brother Lawrence none of my classmates described Brother Ralph as tough, yet he ran a very disciplined, orderly 8A. He could quickly put you in your place if need be, and did so often in a witty, verbal exchange which left his adversaries in line and humbled.

I experienced this firsthand. For some unknown reason, my mother had had it with my manic eleven-year-old behavior and threatened to take me before our new pastor, Father Matt Kelly, who would set me on the correct path. Could it have been due to my attempt to re-varnish our dining room table and, in the process, ruining it and destroying the linoleum flooring under it with spilled paint and varnish remover? Could her anger have been related to my habit of heating Kiwi wax shoe polish in its can to soften it and then almost setting our apartment on fire as it burned through and destroyed the finish on our landlord's kitchen range? Tommy Luhmann and I used to polish our shoes together every Saturday afternoon. He lived in the apartment under ours on Ralph Avenue, and he had suggested the heating of the shoe polish. Could it have been due to the report Mammy heard from other mothers that all of our gang had been spotted dropping raw eggs from the Gates Avenue El train on the pedestrians below walking on Broadway — even though we never did manage to hit anyone? Or could it have related to the time when I and a bunch of fellow altar boys — including Johnny McClorey and Pat Walsh — had consumed a fair amount of unconsecrated Communion hosts, as well as some unconsecrated altar wine? We got caught doing so in the sacristy at Our Lady of Good

Counsel by the old Irish sacristan, who "squealed" on us and pointed to me as the ringleader. (As punishment we had to sell the local Catholic newspaper — *The Tablet* — after all the Sunday Masses for the next month, and were deprived of the one-cent profit on each paper, which retailed for ten cents). Who knows what the reason was? Perhaps my sisters Helen or Bunny will eventually reveal the REAL reasons for Mammy's upset.

Father Kelly referred the "problem" to Brother Ralph and Brother Robert (who taught a different section of 8B that year), both of whom took me aside to discuss the situation. Both quietly but forcefully spoke to me, and my incorrigibility soon corrected itself. The road to perdition lay behind; in front loomed adolescence and the distant realm of adulthood and maturity.

In each of the higher grades (fifth through eighth) a music appreciation class, held once a week for one hour, equipped all of us with high culture — but at the outrageous rate of ten cents per week! The music teacher, Miss Hessian, must have been in her late seventies. A tall formal woman, she was immaculately attired but utterly incapable of disciplining any of us who almost universally hated the attempts to give us some "couth and culture." Her class generally entailed singing old Stephen Foster songs, humming the music scales, and memorizing the birth-death dates of Ludwig Van Beethoven and Johann Sebastian Bach. We were more interested in "The Chattanoogie Shoe Shine Boy," "On Top of Old Smokey," and the early beginnings of rock 'n' roll. I can't fathom how she survived the mayhem of these classes. I guess she needed the income. It could have been worse. The girls' school of Our Lady of Good Counsel had to study art instead of music, again at the usurious rate of ten cents a week! Music was bad enough. How would we have survived art?

The other cultured feature of Our Lady of Good Counsel school life entailed a periodic movie, usually about some Italian saint, usually featuring actors and actresses speaking Italian with some unintelligible English dubbed in. This also cost us ten cents a week, but we didn't mind this too much since it got us out of class and we watched these cinematic gems with the girls. By the seventh and eighth grades, this became a definite positive in our cultural formation since we began noticing the girls! Peter Fiorillo recalls that one of the films the school showed over and over was *The Jackie Robinson Story*, actually one of the best films featured at Our Lady of Good Counsel. When it was shown, ever recurring arguments and fights in the auditorium's balcony actually ceased because all of us paid strict attention to it, particularly in view of the fact that all of us were rabid Brooklyn Dodger fans. Johnny McClorey remembers *St. Rose of Lima*, shown three times—in Italian; *Our Lady of Fatima*, shown twice; and the ever-popular silent version of

The King of Kings, shown at least five times, mostly during Lent.

In summing up these years, let me add a few more anecdotes.

One of the incidents I recall from the fourth grade relates to the somewhat bizarre behavior of a fellow student whom I will call Tommy Elderts. He would drink the ink at his desk! Back then our school desks had an inkwell in the upper right corner. Occasionally the school's staff would fill these wells with ink for those students who used a fountain pen. Most of us filled our pens with our own ink, which we carried in a small Scripto jar. Whatever the ink's origin, Tommy would drink it, smearing it all over his mouth and hands to the shocked surprise of both Miss Mitchell and the entire class. One day, when he made a total mess of everything, our teacher sent him to the principal's office and we never saw him again. With hindsight I recall that Tommy displayed other symptoms of mental anguish: he frequently lost his temper; he cursed at whoever ticked him off; he frequently failed to appear for classes. Perhaps he disappeared to a mental hospital. Perhaps he transferred to P.S. 26, the infamous public elementary school two blocks away. Perhaps he had been exiled to Long Island. Sixty years later I can still recall his ink-smeared face as he sat at his desk two rows ahead of mine.

In the sixth grade, a new boy named Carmine arrived in one of the other class sections. He had just immigrated to the United States with his family, having survived the chaos in Italy during and after World War II. Carmine could test anyone's patience since his loud, ungrammatical, broken English frequently interrupted our conversations or made demands we didn't understand. Even for all his awkwardness, he fit in reasonably well. However, another kid whom I will call Dexter Bryon decided to fool Carmine. Dexter brought a box of chocolate Ex-Lax to class and offered it to the unsuspecting Carmine who consumed the entire box, thinking the contents were chocolate candies. The results could have been catastrophic since the victim had to be hospitalized for more than a week. He survived and his parents came to the school and in harsh broken English lashed out at the principal, the teachers, and obviously the culprit. The new pastor, Father Kelly, became involved and things calmed down. Since Carmine and Dexter were in different sixth-grade sections, I don't know the final outcome, but Dexter probably suffered a few weeks' suspension. He did graduate with the rest of us two years later. Carmine survived his ordeal, but he and his family moved from the area a year later.

A third incident involved a fellow classmate whom I will call Billy Turner. Billy had the unfortunate habit of urinating in his pants in class on a daily basis. This became very disturbing, not only for this poor fellow, but for the students who occupied desks close to his. The problem became even more noticeable when our seventh-grade teacher, Brother Demas, noticed that Billy's urine gradually was eating away the varnish on his chair. To make matters worse, Brother Demas constantly mocked Billy. The rest of us sometimes joined in this mocking, but usually avoided any contact with Billy. So much for even a minimal understanding of his problem. Obviously this problem for a seventh grader demanded some medical or psychological intervention. Today virtually any teacher or staff member would see that the pants wetting was involuntary and out of the boy's immediate control. Then many simply viewed it as a controllable oddity. Billy also transferred out of our class and I have no recollection of his fate.

A fourth incident took place in the eighth grade when Georgie James carved his name in large letters on his desk and colored them with blue-black ink. When discovered, Georgie claimed someone else did it. Now normally that would have meant that the vandal would have been expelled, probably spending the remainder of that grade at P.S. 26. But Brother Ralph handled it very well. He summoned Georgie's parents to a conference with our principal, Brother Stanislas, and said that if the desk top were removed, sanded down and re-varnished, there would be no further punishment.

Georgie's parents accepted the decision and had the desk top restored, so much so that it clearly outshone all the other desks. Georgie also graduated with us months later, but I suppose he had to deal with his irate parents for a while after his vandalism.

The fifth incident was the saddest of all. One of the students, Frankie, could only be considered a loner. He never quite mixed with the other Our Lady of Good Counsel kids, yet he was an altar boy and if I'm not mistaken, a choir boy as well. A grade ahead of me, he lived with his widowed mother and her aunt. One spring morning, all of us learned that Frankie had murdered his mother and aunt, with an axe no less, and refused to give the police a reason why he had done so. Father McCabe had the difficult job of administering the Last Rites and tried to speak to Frankie and console him. We never heard anything more about him other than that he'd been sent to a mental hospital.

The Parish and Its Programs

As the neighborhood descended further into crime and violence, we found refuge in a myriad of parish activities. Upsetting incidents of crime—the sexual assault of a young mother of the parish, the murder of Otto the shoemaker, the robbery of the owner of Cheap Charlie's comic books store, the increasing violence with the gangs in the area, the burglaries of shops on Ralph Avenue—made life more difficult for everyone. The parish church and school's auditorium provided a welcome respite from the anxieties now besetting all of my group. Gradually our lives began to revolve around the religious and social outlets provided to us, usually under the sponsorship of Father F.X. McCabe or Father Matt Kelly. The events they created were a welcome antidote to the increasing neighborhood anarchy. These two priests organized most of the youth activities, and both originally served under Monsignor Philip Brady, the pastor of Our Lady of Good Counsel and an interesting character. Pastors in those days held absolute power, and the Irish ones used it unsparingly. Their decisions were final and few ever questioned them in even minor issues. I recall one story about Monsignor Brady. In the mid-1940s, the Knights of Columbus organized a St. Patrick's Day dinner-dance in the school's auditorium. It was a semiformal event complete with a small orchestra. All was ready the night of the dance and the auditorium filled with parishioners and guests, all awaiting the arrival of Monsignor Brady, who was escorted by uniformed Knights with their swords, capes, and plumed hats. Over the stage hung a banner emblazoned with the words "Happy St. Paddy's Day." When the pastor entered, he saw the banner and became livid and announced to all that the term "Paddy" desecrated the saint's name. Outraged, he dismissed the entire assembly. Yes, he threw everyone out! Like scared sheep, all left the auditorium, none challenging his prerogatives or authority. In those days that's how pastors ruled their flocks. Fortunately those times are long since gone and Father Devanney, and eventually Father Kelly, assumed the helm after Monsignor Brady's death. Both ran things in a far more democratic manner.

Many of my classmates became either altar boys or choir boys. The altar boys of Our Lady of Good Counsel definitely claimed a higher status than the choir boys. Virtually all of our gang became altar boys, which meant memorizing all the Latin responses in the Mass as well as mastering all the rituals required in serving Mass, Benediction, funerals, and weddings. Monthly, each of us received our assignments from Father McCabe as to which Mass we would serve. Often this entailed the daily 6:30 a.m. Mass, which each of us served for a full week. On one such occasion, in the dark of winter, I arose from my slumber at 2:15 a.m. Thinking it was 6:15, I trudged to the church, only to discover it was locked. I couldn't think what was wrong until I looked across Putnam Avenue and noticed that the clock in Phelan's Funeral Home registered 2:25! Back home I went for four more hours of fitful sleep before setting off again at 6:15.

Two annual rituals of my altar boy days remain in my memory: Forty Hours Devotion and Palm Sunday. In Our Lady of Good Counsel, Forty Hours Devotion took place every February and started on a Friday evening and finished on Sunday afternoon. It consisted of homilies by the priests, recitation of the Holy Rosary, nightly Benediction, and Adoration of the Blessed Sacrament. What sticks with me however was the annual "fight" between the altar and choir boys on the Saturday night following the closing Benediction. It really wasn't much of a true fight but a sort of turf war. It consisted of a snowball attack on the choir boys as they exited the school where they had changed their choir robes. Since we altar boys outnumbered the "wimpish" choir boys, we always won the contest and jeered at our victims as they ran, snow covered, from the area.

The Palm Sunday memory focuses on the night before the feast day, when we prepared the palm branches for Sunday's Masses. This entailed twenty to twenty-five altar boys stripping individual palm leaves from larger stalks and arranging them neatly for the next morning's distribution to the hundreds of people who appeared for the Palm Sunday liturgy, many of whom had not been to church since Christmas. After the palms were stripped, we had a ball attacking each other with them. Getting whacked by a handful of palms definitely stung, yet no one ever really got hurt.

In payment for services rendered to Our Lady of Good Counsel during the year, Father McCabe organized various outings for the altar boys, choir boys, girls' societies, and helpers at the summer Bible Vacation School. This generally involved a trip to the CYO camp at Coney Island for a day's lark in the sun and surf. Off we would go — forty or fifty kids — traveling on the Jamaica El, transferring at Eastern Parkway for the A train, transferring again at Franklin Avenue, to take another train to Prospect Park station, until we made the final ride on the Brighton Express to Stillwell Avenue/Coney Island. Then we walked about a mile carrying blankets, towels, and lunches, finally arriving at our destination. After a day in the sun, most of us were totally sunburned, exhausted from maneuvering around the debris in Coney Island's surf, flat broke after spending our nickels and dimes at the Wonder Wheel, the Cyclone, the Whip, and the bumper cars, fighting indigestion following the consumption of Nathan's famous hot dogs and Nedick's orange drink. After all this we retraced our train rides in subway cars totally jammed and roasting with the heat, standing all the way in wet bathing suits encrusted with scourging sand. We usually got home around 8 p.m. But it was great fun!

Father McCabe had a special treat on one of these ventures. He arranged for all the boys and girls in the group to have a spaghetti and meatball dinner at Coney Island's famous Gargiulo's Restaurant. Mind you, this blew our minds since most of us had never eaten in a restaurant up to that point. For the occasion, we changed our wet bathing suits for proper dinner clothes after a cold shower at the CYO camp. I can still remember where I sat at a long table and how delicious the meal of spaghetti and meatballs were. All of us brought additional "formal" clothes for such a spectacular event and all agreed that it was one of the real highlights of our young lives—even though the sunburned Irish kids among us sat at the dinner table in quiet agony.

On another CYO Coney Island excursion, my mother told me to make sure I took care of my sister Helen who was age nine at the time, being careful not to lose her in the crowds at the beach. I kept an eye on her all day, but, sure enough, I did lose her when we were returning to the subway for the ride home. I assumed that she was with her friends and didn't give it a thought until I arrived home. Mammy said, "Where's your sister?" I replied that the last time I saw her was at the Nathan's stand. After waiting about an hour, my mom became frantic and we started the search for Helen. Mammy was about to go back to Coney Island when the police from the 81st Precinct arrived to tell us that Helen was safe and sound, currently in the Coney Island Precinct. Helen became separated from our larger group of fifty kids. She'd been weakened after the day's trip and by carrying her wet towels (and I'm embarrassed to say, mine, which I told her to carry). Finally, she got "lost" around Nathan's. Fortunately, Helen found a police officer and told him she was lost. He took her to the station house, where two detectives brought her to a local diner for a roast beef sandwich and ice cream. When my mom arrived, frantic with fear, she found Helen calmly and happily downing the last of her ice cream. After that escapade I was grounded for quite some time. Helen delights in telling this story, one in which I do not emerge a hero. I'm sure she will recount the sordid details to anyone who inquires about the event.

In the parish, there were a number of additional groups which attracted the boys in my group. All of us joined the Columbian Squires, the junior division of the Knights of Columbus. Some joined the Junior Holy Name Society, the teenage version of the larger group of adult males in the parish. Most of our group joined the Boy Scouts under Headmaster Daly, an ex-marine who became a role model for many. (I did not actually join the scouts because my mom could not afford the eleven dollars for a scout's uniform.) Mr. Daly, however, invited me to all the activities of the troop because I had a stamp collection and he prided himself on his own stamp collection. Since my mother worked cleaning offices at the New York Cotton Exchange on Wall Street, she brought me all kinds of foreign stamps from the mail there. So I fit in nicely with our local troop of scouts without having to pass my Tenderfoot test, with its ordeal of demonstrating, among other feats, the tying of the infamous sheepshank knot.

Of these various groups, the one which I enjoyed most was the Columbian Squires. Our adult mentor, Ben Palagonia, represented the Knights and truly gave his all to organizing our Squire's circle, a monthly meeting of the teen members which provided educational, cultural, and spiritual activities. The Knights of Columbus council of the parish formed the Squires with the aim of encouraging the young male teens to consider becoming knights as they matured. Our group—the Peter Richard Circle—met monthly on the top floor of the boys' school at Our Lady of Good Counsel to conduct Circle business, which usually involved a formal education program followed by a sports/recreation activity. Over a three-year period, our Chief Squires included Johnny McClorey, Peter Fiorillo, and Pat Walsh. Victor Herbert, Pat Connelly, and I served at various times as deputy chief squires. On an ever-changing basis, Victor headed the Spiritual Committee along with Joe Morra and Joey Walsh; Louis Mione ran the Social Committee, assisted by Robbie Bogart (who also was the circle's notary), and Bop Jones and I arranged the Civic-Cultural Committee, with Richie Heraty as our sentry. (Why we needed a sentry eludes me. Perhaps we were expecting a raid by the Chaplains or the El Quintos gangs.) Two other Squires served as treasurers. Interestingly, both were very active gamblers who lost more than they won. No wonder our treasury was always empty. Highlights of our "lectures" included:

1. Victor Herbert talking about St. Joseph Cupertino, who Victor claimed was the patron saint of "those in doubt of passing," which probably would have included the entire group of Squires whose ranks numbered nineteen members, according to one of Chief Squire McClorey's monthly reports.

2. Louis Mione attempting to raise money for our depleted treasury by organizing the Social Committee to sell candy known as Mrs. Leland's Butter Bits, an effort that ultimately netted fifty dollars.

3. Joe Morra organizing the bowling team, which competed in the Columbian Squires International Bowling Tournament, an effort that ultimately... well, why don't I skip to the next program?

4. Mike Rockwood, Louis Mione, and Robbie Bogart organizing the track team, which competed in the Annual Columbian Squires Track Meet for New York City where we failed to win any medals or trophies. (All agreed the judges were very biased against us.)

5. Frankie Becallo presenting a slide show of our Chief Counselor Ben Palagonia's trip to Jamestown and Yorktown, Virginia, highlighting the historical features of each community.

6. Our debate teams weighing in on the pros and cons of segregation in response to what was then the recent integration of Little Rock, Arkansas schools. The integration team included Victor Herbert, Joe Morra, and Richie Heraty; the segregation team comprised Johnny McClorey, Pat Connelly, and me. Our segregation team won by a score of 225 to 200. Years later, I wonder, *What were we thinking? What in heaven's name could the arguments have been?* Yet, back in 1957 this was a burning issue across the nation. I only wish that I had been on the integration team and that the integration arguments had prevailed.

7. Ben Palagonia lecturing on the History of Flight, complete with blackboard diagrams, and my lecture on the History of World War II covering both the Pacific and European theaters. Each lecture lasted 45 minutes!

Besides the usual programs, a few excursions took place—to Bear Mountain, the Museum of Natural History, and the Hayden Planetarium. But our best trip entailed a weekend campout which Ben Palagonia arranged in a desolate area of Patchogue, Long Island. He borrowed tents from some of the Knights so twelve of us could spend a Friday night camping, most of us for the first time. Because of fears of bears (on Long Island?), nasty mosquitoes, and cold weather, none of us slept. But Mr. Palagonia slept like a baby in his tent. He had tethered his large black Labrador to its main pole. As a practical joke, some of the group—most likely Heraty, Connelly, and Pat Walsh—decided to lure the dog to them, offering the animal some of their Dinty Moore Stew. The dog charged the bowl, pulling Palagonia's tent after him. Well, that did it. The next morning Palagonia said the trip was over, and we all went home a day earlier than we'd planned. So much for the wilderness. Years later I marvel at Palagonia's patience with us. He truly gave his all to our group and put up with all sorts of nonsense, serving as a generous and unrewarded role model for many of us. An architect, he introduced us to the professional world with his mentoring of our committee, his interest in current events, his encouragement of public speaking and group organization, and his patience with a group of fairly wild teenagers.

Now it may strike the reader as curious why so much of my life and those of my friends revolved around Our Lady of Good Counsel. Today, Catholic youth still belong to a local parish, but youth involvement is probably limited to Sunday Mass; Confraternity of Christian Doctrine, or CCD, classes; perhaps a teen group; and some summer volunteer work project. Remember, however, that my group had little chance to join anything outside the parish simply because few, if any, activities presented themselves. Kids today have town recreation programs that sponsor everything from basketball and baseball to art lessons and theater classes. Schools offer all sorts of extracurricular activities. Lives are infinitely more geographically mobile than mine was. Our lives literally revolved almost entirely around our section of Bedford Stuyvesant, with very rare trips to Manhattan, which was scarcely five miles away.

Our Lady of Good Counsel became our lifeline, our connection to something larger than Jefferson Avenue and Hancock Street. There we met and established friendships with other teens and our horizons broadened ever so slightly. There, to varying degrees, we became Roman Catholics and breathed the air of Catholicism, particularly the Irish version of it. We learned how to behave as adolescents and eventually as adults — for better or worse. Here also Our Lady of Good Counsel provided "employment" for all my group, some of it paid, most of it voluntary.

Many of us worked in the parish for one dollar a week (and a free bottle of Coca-Cola) setting up the auditorium for weekly Thursday night Bingo and taking down the tables and chairs each Saturday for Sunday Mass. Jim Kearney, two years older than I, served as our boss and he, like a proverbial Tammany Hall politician, doled out the dollars and cokes after we completed our week on Saturdays. It's remarkable we even got the task accomplished since approximately fifteen of us were so employed and more time was spent goofing off than actually working. One of our non-work games involved dividing our gang into two groups, one stationed in the balcony of the auditorium, the other on its floor. Each group had carpet guns—homemade wooden pistols with a large rubber band attached. They were loaded individually with one-inch square pieces of discarded floor linoleum used as ammunition to fire at the opposition. Occasionally, we substituted bent paper clips as ammunition. One fateful time, this "bullet" struck me and lodged in my right eyelid. Luckily, I had blinked before it hit so there was no lasting damage. My group still loves to talk of these fun-filled times.

Most of us also volunteered as teen leaders in the parish's Summer Bible School, teaching catechism, showing younger kids how to make key chains and lariats, organizing games such as dodgeball and Chinese handball, serving lunches of peanut butter and carrot sandwiches provided by the city's board of education, and helping chaperone group excursions to the CYO camp in Coney Island. As we slowly became aware of the opposite sex, we also participated in all sorts of social outlets, generally organized by Rosie Welsher, Jo Pallazzo, Mary Kearney, Judy O'Donnell, and my sister Helen. Victor Herbert also organized numerous skits and short plays where each of us tried out our acting skills, or lack thereof.

One such skit, directed by Victor, involved a pseudo-surgery scene. On the auditorium's stage, he suspended several white cotton sheets. Behind these a group of us stood over a table with a "patient" on it, mimicking an actual surgery. Behind the "operations" he placed several lamps with very bright bulbs so that the audience saw an operation only in silhouette form. We surgeons yelled for sutures, scalpels, blood transfusions, and bandages as we pulled out ropes, chains, and pieces of pottery from the patient's abdomen. Remarkably the patient—probably Pat Connelly—survived, long enough to take his bow and relish the cheers from the appreciative audience.

Victor, a true thespian, continually thought of new skits and brief plays which he ably produced and directed. One notable short act play (the name of which I can't remember) involved the patriotic theme of the Fourth of July. Its closing scene involved the sighting of the nation's mascot—a bald eagle. When it appeared in silhouette form, Ernie Melendez was supposed to exclaim, "Look, look, a bald-headed eagle!" Instead, in his excitement, he yelled in Spanish, "*Mira, mira,* a bald-headed eagle!" The house erupted with laughter and applause. Multiculturalism and diversity were slowly taking root.

Often the Squires joined with the Junior Holy Name Society to sponsor teen dances in the parish hall. These dances featured rock and roll music, provided by the teenage girls on 45 rpm records and played over the auditorium's speaker system.

Often about one hundred teens attended these dances. Occasionally, problems arose. At one Sunday afternoon dance, a group of local Puerto Rican boys "crashed the dance." We enlisted the toughest boy in our group to confront them and tell the interlopers to leave. They refused and suggested that their best fighter and our champion fight it out in the school's yard to see who'd win. We welcomed the fight since no one had ever beaten the tough Tommy.

When the two groups emerged in the yard, the two antagonists squared off for the fight, whereupon the Puerto Rican teen kicked Tommy in the groin, punched his stomach, and threw him to the pavement where he started pounding his head on the concrete. Horrified, Blackie Molloy and I stopped the fight to prevent further injury to Tommy. All agreed that the interlopers be admitted to the dance and they calmly did so, creating no further problems. Tommy, fully shaken by the encounter in which he never saw what hit him, pulled himself together and rejoined the rest of us at the dance, which went on as if nothing had happened. Following this encounter, Tommy never became involved in physical fights again, whereas before, he sought out battles. You might say he became "gun shy," avoiding confrontation where he might be pummeled again.

Besides our social activities within the parish, another of our main forms of recreation involved our weekly visit to Mario's Pizza Parlor. Rundown, seedy, and lit with one fluorescent light over the main seating area, Mario's became a place where we could hang out and consume what then was a novel new food—a pizza pie. In the mid-1950s, a sixteen-inch pizza cost one dollar, certainly affordable for most of us who pooled our nickels and dimes to purchase one. Usually six of us would share a pie. Yet Mario never cut the slices evenly, so there might be a large piece, and several irregularly shaped smaller slices. Our solution as to who got which piece entailed spinning the pizza tray. Whatever piece stopped in front of you was yours. This democratic method worked well—unless Mickey sat with you. Mickey, who had a few screws loose, would SPIT on the largest slice, disgusting everyone with him. But they all gladly relinquished any claim to that slice. Perhaps this practice befitted the milieu of the "restaurant" since Mario often remarked to us that if a customer ticked him off, he would spit in the salad he prepared in the kitchen for the unwary customer.

Peter Fiorillo reminded me that all of our gang had been invited to Mario's wedding, which was celebrated in the back of a local bar. You paid either five or ten dollars to attend, depending on your financial state. The admission entitled you to the "football wedding" culinary fare—cold-cut sandwiches wrapped in wax paper and thrown to you by the server. Hence the term "football wedding."

Peter didn't remain long at the wedding since the hall overflowed with drunken revelers celebrating Mario's new role in life. I have no memory of attending the wedding.

Though all of us Squires enjoyed our meetings, excursions, and thematic "lectures," our greatest thrill consisted of playing floor hockey following the formal parts of our meetings. This game was totally improvised. We played it on the gym-like floor on the third floor of the boys' school at Our Lady of Good Counsel, which had a slippery surface well suited to players who removed their shoes or sneakers and "skated" in stocking/sock feet. The goals consisted of two folding chairs at each end of the floor, with an eight-foot space between each "goal post." A felt blackboard eraser served as the puck. Each team, without any plans of action or method, tried to kick the eraser into the opponent's goal. There was only one problem: the opposite player would also try to kick the puck away from you, and many fateful collisions occurred when each combatant kicked simultaneously at the eraser. I still recall the pain.

This commenced my lifelong issue with foot problems, specifically chronically infected ingrown toenails on my large toe on each foot. Eventually, by age eighteen, I needed foot surgery. The first time, our family physician, Dr. George Bodkin, told me he had to operate on my right foot to cure the problem, which he did at St. Catherine's Hospital.

When I awoke from the operation, I noticed both feet were heavily bandaged. When Doc Bodkin made his rounds, I asked, "Why both feet?" He remarked I would have had problems with the left foot in the future but he didn't want to tell me beforehand lest I cancel the surgery. So I hobbled around on crutches for three weeks! The surgery worked well, but almost fifteen years later, the problem returned on the right foot, necessitating new surgery. That operation seems to have solved the problem and, as long as I avoid Squire floor hockey, I should be OK.

Getting back to Our Lady of Good Counsel floor hockey, one night our group decided to play, but the school was dark and locked. Peter Fiorillo picked the main lock. We decided not to play on the third floor since the lights there would reveal our clandestine presence. Instead we played in the basement where no windows would betray us. We made so much noise, however, that Father Devanney heard us and came over from the rectory to throw us out. For the next four Sundays, all of us were required to hand out the church bulletins following each of the Sunday Masses, not an unduly harsh punishment for a bunch of teenage trespassers, though Peter felt we should have been paid at least a nominal fee for our efforts.

By late 1957, the neighborhood had slowly descended even further into urban blight. Living on Ralph Avenue, where we'd moved from Halsey

Street, became impossible because arson suddenly befell our building. The ground floor of 84 Ralph Avenue had been an ice cream/candy store but the owner simply wasn't making it. One night around midnight, we and another family in the two apartments above the store were alerted by a passerby that the store was afire! Quickly all the residents awakened and abandoned the site, which was moderately damaged, mainly by smoke. Later fire marshalls determined the fire to have been of suspicious origin. Suspicious? We never doubted a "torch" had been hired. The going rate then was $200 per fire to burn the store so the owner could collect insurance, but we never could prove it. It's what was called URVA (urban renewal via arson).

For the next few months, rats occupied the gutted store, frightening all of us living above. We saw ten to fifteen of them at a time scurrying throughout the back yard. My sisters and I, having viewed so many of the same medieval knight Hollywood films, decided to boil water in pots and pour it from our third-floor window on the unsuspecting rats below—just as besieged knights did from their castle ramparts using boiling oil. Yet the sound of the descending water spooked the rats and we failed to kill even one.

Our Uncle Dan, my father's brother who'd arrived as an immigrant from Ireland, solved the problem. He descended at once to the store's basement, which had been blacked out. In the darkness, he simply grabbed fleeing rats and squeezed them, killing them with his bare hands! He killed at least ten that way before he had us purchase rat poison, which eliminated the remaining rodents. Coming from a farm in Ireland he claimed that this constituted the normal way to control rats. Decades later, I still marvel at his nonchalant attitude and his bravery at being able to squeeze a rat to death.

But the rats did it for the O'Kanes living in the old neighborhood. My mom found an apartment in Ozone Park in Queens, and life on Jefferson, Halsey, and Ralph faded into memory. We moved to bucolic, quiet, non-violent Queens. But we only lasted there two years since the new apartment on Atlantic Avenue and 86th Street certainly left much to be desired. It lacked heat, which we had to provide via kerosene stoves, and it lacked hot water, which had to be supplied by a gas-powered heating unit in the kitchen. The apartment had a toilet but no bathroom sink or shower or tub. In winter, the water in the toilet literally froze, and each morning either my sisters or I had to pour boiling water into the bowl to thaw it. It's remarkable that we didn't crack the toilet itself with such a procedure. It was cold in winter and the insulation was so meager that the curtains actually fluttered in the constant drafts. The next door neighbor was an old lady who stockpiled newspapers floor to ceiling. Above us lived a woman and two daughters, and on the top floor lived an old Russian couple. The husband would regularly beat up his wife and lock her out and she would sit howling on the stairs. He also chopped wood in the backyard, and always seemed to carry a small axe. We kept our distance from him. What a place! Mammy said we should have been paid to live there. I presume young readers will wonder if any place like this really existed, but it did. In fact the decrepit building is still there, on Atlantic Avenue, near 86th Street.

Fed up with an abode that would have rivaled the worst cold-water flat anywhere, we moved back to Brooklyn, but to a good section of town. This time we found an apartment at 216 Cleveland Street in East New York, in a large comfortable Italian-American neighborhood. Since the area was "mobbed up with Mafiosi," street crime simply did not exist; the "boys" ("goodfellas") would take care of any "difficulties." Yet things always change. At this writing that area in the 75th Precinct records the highest homicide rate in all of New York City and has had that unfortunate distinction for the past fifteen years. One media report stated the precinct is the most dangerous in the world. During our time there it was far more peaceful. We lived on Cleveland Street for approximately four years before we moved yet again to a more spacious apartment at 1206 Cortelyou Road in the Flatbush section. I resided there till I met and married my wife Margaret and moved to Park Slope and eventually to New Jersey. But that's another story which comes years later.

Following our graduation from Our Lady of Good Counsel's elementary school, my group entered the storm of adolescence, a period of life few people would choose to repeat. As usual, the peer group played a seminal role in our maturation and expanded beyond the Jefferson Avenue gang to include Pat Walsh, Victor Herbert, Richie Heraty, Pat Connelly, Kenny McNally, Richie Howe, Mike Rockwood, Frankie Winters, as well as many others who lived on the adjacent streets. Virtually all had been classmates at Our Lady of Good Counsel. Though most of us attended different high schools (Bishop Loughlin Memorial, St. John's Prep, Bushwick, Cathedral Prep Seminary, St. Francis Prep, Franklin K. Lane), we kept our group intact during our teenage years. We "practiced" becoming men, and on the streets we learned to smoke, drink, participate in organized sports, and play all forms of poker.

For any budding adolescent in Brooklyn in the early 1950s, smoking was virtually obligatory. Every older adolescent smoked and most carried the pack of cigarettes in the rolled sleeve of their sparkling white T-shirts. Often they would purchase individual cigarettes (called "loosies") at the candy store on Ralph Avenue rather than pay for a new complete pack. "Grubbing a smoke" from others constituted a way of life for some too cheap to buy their own. A grubber would approach and ask for a cigarette, claiming he'd pay you back in a day or two, but the payback never happened. To avoid loaning cigarettes, you kept two packs with you. The first, generally full, was concealed in your pants pocket. The second, visible on your T-shirt arm, had only one cigarette in it. When asked, you would exclaim, "This is my last smoke, and I can't do without it." This always worked, and the grubber would have to seek out new prey.

To master the art and science of smoking, our group assembled on the roof of Pat Walsh's apartment house to practice. Johnny McClorey advised everyone to lie flat on the roof, so no pedestrians below would see our silhouettes with the tell-tale smoke trail giving away our activity.

For some reason I can't recall, I missed this smoking apprenticeship session and felt totally isolated and rejected, since I hadn't learned to smoke, and more importantly, I couldn't inhale like the others. I was both dejected and determined to remedy the situation. So a few days after the practice session, I waited until my mom and sisters left our apartment to spend an afternoon with Aunt Mildred and her family, and the coast was clear. Only my grandma was home, but she was too infirm even to notice my plan. With no trouble I purchased a full pack of Camels and reasoned that if I inhaled every cigarette, I would master the knack, moving upward into the ranks of the veteran smokers in our gang. I closed my hall bedroom door and proceeded to puff and inhale the first cigarette. Slowly but surely, I became deathly sick with dizziness and nausea. I never got beyond that first cigarette! What a failure, at age twelve. It took almost an hour for my senses to return to normal, at which point I tried to conceal my nausea and my pack of smokes from my family, who by that time had returned. My sister Bunny exclaimed, "What's that strange smell? Jamesie, have you been smoking?" My denials convinced no one, and Mammy discovered the pack of Camels in the garbage and subsequently grounded me for the next seventeen years! Yet failure has its untold positive consequences. Almost six decades later, I still become nauseated when I encounter cigarette smoke. So perhaps yesterday's defeat is today's victory.

Consuming alcohol constituted another adolescent rite of passage. In our area virtually everyone drank alcoholic beverages—Rheingold and Schaefer beer, all kinds of Scotches, Seagram's blended whiskeys, Gallo wines, and for those down-and-out winos, Thunderbird, which had to be the bottom of the barrel since it was cheapest fortified wine on the market. ("Thunderbird, what's the price? Thirty twice." That was sixty cents a bottle). Our group chose red wine since we felt it had "class" and "cachet." Our usual choices, Gallo Muscatel or Gallo Port, cost a dollar per bottle and even kids age twelve or thirteen could purchase either with no questions asked.

Often we each would consume an entire bottle and become thoroughly inebriated. Pat Connelly usually suggested a simple answer to our predicament: "Let's go to Katz's luncheonette and drink black coffee." This we did, which quickly sickened us all, resulting in a mess on the sidewalk outside Katz's store. Since this sequence occurred every time we drank wine, these encounters eventually cured us of the excesses of drinking and in time we switched to the less toxic beverage of beer. Most of the time, we purchased either Rheingold or Schaefer because they cost less than other brands. Their jingles replay in my head years later: "My beer is Rheingold, the dry beer. Think of Rheingold whenever you buy beer. It's not bitter, not sweet. It's the extra dry treat. Won't you try extra dry Rheingold beer?" "Schaefer is the one beer to have when you're having more than one. Schaefer pleasure doesn't fade even when your thirst is done."

In the 1950s, Rheingold sponsored the Miss Rheingold Contest. Every subway car hosted pictures of the six beauties vying for the honor of being crowned Miss Rheingold. Any subway rider could vote for his favorite by filling in the ballot appended to the poster. Looking back, I recall that all the contestants looked very Irish, very German, or very WASP. Few were Italian and none were black or Latino, strange as this may have seemed in an increasingly diversified city. I presume that was the main reason the Miss Rheingold contest eventually ceased to exist.

Around the time we began drinking beer, Johnny McClorey, his sister Eileen, and their parents decided to take a week's vacation. But they had a problem—they didn't know what to do with their dog, Spud. Since Johnny's parents admired me (rightfully so!), they said, "Why don't we let Jamesie watch Spud, feed him, and walk him?" I agreed, but Johnny made me swear that I wouldn't let our buddies have a beer party in his apartment. I duly swore, but the gang—particularly Pat Walsh and Pat Connelly—hounded me to have a party. After four days, I finally relented to the pressure and we brought in our six-packs and potato chips. We lounged in the apartment and drank, and after an hour or so Pat Walsh suggested we put some Rheingold in Spud's bowl. Spud devoured it. We gave him more, which he lapped up, and eventually he became blind drunk, slipping and sliding on the floor, falling from the McClorey couch. We howled with laughter and had a grand time. Following the party, we spruced up Johnny's apartment, resetting the traps he had set for us in case we invaded his home (e.g. scotch taped doors which would become undone if we opened them, talcum powder on part of the floor to reveal our multiple footprints), and we made sure Spud sobered up. We looked around and thought we were home free, but when Johnny's mother cleaned the living room a few days later, she discovered a beer can under the living room sofa. Somehow we'd missed it in our attempt to make it appear that no one other than Spud and I had been there. Johnny remained under house arrest for the next few weeks!

As we moved further into adolescence, poker became one of our group's favorite forms of entertainment. We played all kinds of card games—Red Dog, BlackJack, Five Card Stud, and Straight Poker, but Seven Card Stud became the game of choice which could accommodate up to seven players. I preferred BlackJack (or "21," as we called it) since you could bet scientifically (never take a hit with sixteen; hold your cards with seventeen). If you had "the bank," you were in the catbird seat since, in a tie, the bank always won. The "banker" was chosen randomly; the player who held the highest card in a random deal had the right to hold "the bank." The only times I avoided BlackJack were when Johnny McClorey held the bank since he played the odds extremely well and could read the eyes of those bluffing very well. He usually cleaned out the rest of us rather quickly. We always gambled for money at these games. Seven Card Stud provided the most fun, since so many of us could play, bluff, and try to cheat. Generally, no one person did well bluffing or cheating until midnight, which we all agreed beforehand would be the end time for the game. That was all well and good for those who might be winning at that point, but the losers would become very angry since they had no time to recoup their losses. To keep peace we would extend the closing time to 12:30 a.m. True to form, the losers would start bluffing, making poor choices in their bets, yelling and screaming, and usually ending up broke. If you used your head, memorized the statistical odds on an inside straight, three of a kind, or a full house, it was difficult for you to lose even though I did on numerous occasions. It's all a science, provided you play with others who rely on bluff to baffle their opponent.

On one memorable evening, both McClorey and I lost early in the Five Card Open match. Mike Rockwood and Pat Walsh wiped us out, with Kenny McNally, Pat Connelly, Peter Fiorillo, and Richie Heraty struggling to break even.

We all had a deal: whoever lost early in the poker match would have to take food orders from the rest of the pack, collect the costs, and go to the local White Castle restaurant on Atlantic Avenue (near McClorey's new apartment in East New York) and purchase hamburgers for everyone. So McClorey and I trudged the four blocks to the White Castle. Even though he lost his money in the poker game, McClorey's optimistic sense of humor shone. He approached the counter of the grand eatery and asked, "Are hamburgers sold here?" The lady said, "Yes, and each costs eleven cents." The paltry, pathetic burgers were quite small, with five circular holes in each. McClorey, the connoisseur, said he would buy one and taste it, which he did. He said, "O'Kane, this is great!" Then he told the woman he wanted fifty-five additional burgers to go! Thinking him a wise guy, the woman called the manager who practically evicted us from the Castle. Only after McClorey paid in advance for all fifty-five burgers did they fry them. On leaving the shop, McClorey stated quite loudly, "Jamesie, this is great—fifty-five burgers between us." The store personnel must have thought us crazy. The rest of the gang were delighted to have their burgers—eight per person, minus the one McClorey consumed at the White Castle. The card game progressed, with Mike Rockwood winning the lion's share of the group's money, and Kenny McNally losing everything on ill-advised bluffing as the clock neared midnight. A loss for McClorey and O'Kane, but at least we had some fun at the White Castle.

Beside Johnny McClorey, Mike Rockwood played brilliant poker. I dreaded when Mike held the bank in BlackJack, since he was difficult to outwit. I believe that he had natural brilliance and I considered him the smartest member of our gang. Others disagreed because he had dropped out of Franklin K. Lane High School at age sixteen, the minimal age necessary to legally opt out of the educational system in New York City. I remember the day he dropped out. As Mike retold us later that afternoon, he was called to the school's principal's office, along with eight to ten other students who had indicated they wanted to drop out. All had turned sixteen that same day. (At almost 5,000 students, Franklin K. Lane was one of the largest high schools in the city system. On any given school day ten to fifteen students chose to drop out on their sixteenth birthday). When all had assembled in the principal's outer office, Lane's vice principal appeared, wheeled in an iron birthday cake, complete with one electric candle! Imagine, the kids didn't even warrant a real birthday cake, complete with sixteen real wax candles. All sang "Happy Birthday" and "blew out" the electric candle, at which point the vice principal handed Mike and the others their official papers and told them that if they didn't get off school property immediately, they'd be considered trespassers. This bothered Mike little since he wanted no further part of schooling and couldn't wait to leave. Subsequently, he held a few miserable, go-nowhere jobs in New York's garment district. After a few years floundering, he studied for his high school equivalency degree, took the test, and passed it with flying colors. Eventually, he became a New York City police officer. After that, our gang gradually lost touch with Mike. To this day I still believe him to be the smartest member of the gang, though his paper credentials never quite supported this.

Let me skip ahead a few years to 1958, my first year in college. I continued to play poker with our group and did rather well financially. My winning kept me in cash for pizza money, date expenses, and movie cash. After one all-night game, I financially cleaned out one of my buddies, whom I'll call Billy. Like Mike Rockwood, Billy also had dropped out of high school and worked in the city's garment district pushing clothing racks from one manufacturer to another. For this he received the minimum wage—$40 per week. After taxes, Billy took home $32. At that all-nighter, I won all of Billy's take-home pay. It really bothered me that I won his entire week's wages, even though Billy didn't seem terribly upset by it. I guess you would call this working-class fatalism. That did it for me. After that night, I never played at that level again and took early retirement from poker matches. Some of the perpetual "losers," particularly Blackie Malloy, never quite accepted the fact that I refused to play anymore, but whether or not they realized it, I may have saved them some of their cash. Most of the gang continued gambling and would bet on just about anything, including the horses at Aqueduct Racetrack, college basketball games, random heads-or-tails coin tosses, or high and low temperature changes on a given day. Recently, I learned that one of our group is "in hiding" since he is being pursued by loan sharks seeking payback. As you may have guessed, years earlier that particular friend had been one of the main "bluffers" in our poker matches.

Rewind back to our adolescent years when most of our gang quickly moved beyond the old neighborhood. Even so, we still continued to meet and socialize, sometimes in the old Jefferson Avenue area, other times in areas where some of our group had moved. Since Johnny McClorey and I had moved to the East New York section of Brooklyn, we often convened the group there primarily for touch football games (with blocking, without helmets or padding) in nearby Highland Park, a large tract straddling both Brooklyn and Queens.

On one Saturday in the late fall of 1957, seven of us decided to play football with thirteen teens from that area. In so doing, an issue arose since one of their groups had a kid I'll call "Robbie" as a player. Now Robbie could only be described as a true psychopath. A few months earlier he'd thrown a teenage usher off the balcony of that area's local movie house. The usher had had the temerity to tell Robbie to keep his feet off the seat in front of him. Fortunately, the unlucky usher survived without major injury.

Since we only had seven players, we chose three of their group to play on our side and made sure Robbie was one of those chosen. I quietly whispered to our quarterback, McClorey, to put Robbie in virtually every play, which McClorey gladly did. Now Robbie left much to be desired as a player, but he was quite delighted in his role and relished his newfound "talent." We lost the game, however, which incensed Robbie, who quickly and severely beat one of the other team's players because he had blocked one of Robbie's running plays. Following the game, sensing trouble, our group of seven quickly exited the field. One of our group, however, said, "I'm not running away from anything. It's not their field." For his dalliance, he was jumped by the other group and severely beaten. The rest of us witnessed the trouble from a safe distance. So much for standing on a questionable principle.

Robbie went on to a sordid future. Approximately two years later, he allegedly beat an elderly man to death in Highland Park when the victim chastened him for inappropriate behavior with a young girl. At his trial witnesses changed their testimony and Robbie "beat the rap," but to this day I wonder if he became an enforcer in the Paul Vario mob, located a few avenues away.

Besides playing sports in Highland Park, we ventured well beyond Brooklyn for social purposes. One of our group, Richie Heraty, had moved to Elmont on Long Island. Frequently we traveled by bus to the Jamaica El station to board the subway for our respective home stations. Since we arrived at the station at approximately 2 a.m., there would be a long wait — up to an hour — for the next train to depart. Most of our gang, with the exception of Peter Fiorillo and me, decided to walk the tracks rather than wait. Now I should point out that some were slightly inebriated — though not Peter or I — and walking the tracks, which rose approximately two stories above street level, could be disastrous. Peter and I boarded the train which left the 168th Street station about fifteen minutes after the rest of the group (eight in all) took off on their crazy odyssey. Fortunately, as they could see the train approaching, they jumped to the narrow catwalk and safely watched as the train passed them. But Peter and I did not know they left the tracks for the safety of the catwalk and so assumed the worst. Imagine the *Daily News* headlines: "Eight Teens Killed by Passing Train." We got off at the Sutphin Boulevard station and, to our relief, saw them walking toward us. As they approached the platform, one of them, Pat Walsh, slipped and started falling between the tracks to the street below. To this day he claims that I grabbed and saved him, but honestly, I have no memory of doing so. At any rate, that was the last time any of us walked the tracks.

Gangs and Crime

I n the midst of all this moving in and out of the old neighborhood, one anxiety trumped all other concerns — gang violence. More than any other concern, the fear of gang mayhem permeated my group's behavior not only when all of us lived near Jefferson Avenue, but also when we returned from newer areas to visit those in our group still living there.

Historically, violent gangs constituted a con-tinuing feature of life in New York City, dating as far back as the late 1830s. Famous gangs such as the Dead Rabbits, the Plug Uglies, the Atlantic Guards, the Roach Guards, the Hudson Dusters, the Whyos, the Bowery Boys, the Eastmans, and the Five Pointers are just a few of the more famous New York gangs of the nineteenth and early twentieth centuries. Herbert Asbury's *Gangs of New York* offers a fascinating glimpse of gang violence during that era. Prohibition in the 1920s only fueled the presence and power of the gangs and individual gangsters such as the Legs Diamond, Mad Dog Coll, Albert Anastasia, Meyer Lansky, and Murder Incorporated members (Lepke Buchalter, Gurrah Shapiro, Abe Reles) epitomized the violent nature of that era. But for the most part these gangs comprised adult gangsters, with teens assigned to minor status. The Little Bowery Boys and the Junior Dead Rabbits served their criminal apprenticeship and waited their turn at adult fame. Or should I say infamy?

By the 1940s and certainly the 1950s, however, the prominent gangs in Brooklyn gradually came to comprise teenagers rather than adults. Teens became every bit as violent and unpredictable as their adult counterparts of former eras. This is not to imply that adult gangs had disappeared; they'd morphed into the more stabilized factions of organized crime, led primarily by Jews and Italians and, to a lesser extent, the Irish. Our neighborhood and the surrounding areas in Bedford-Stuyvesant, and the contiguous areas of Brownsville, Fort Greene, Ocean Hill, and Bushwick boasted their respective teen gangs, each vying for notoriety and status within the larger area.

The dominant gang in Brooklyn in the 1950s was the Chaplains, subdivided into two major groups—the Brevoort Project Chaplains and the Fort Greene Chaplains. Interestingly, public housing, known as "the projects," spawned these gangs. Originally envisioned as a major step in ameliorating urban poverty, these publicly subsidized projects actually fueled the violence of that area. A much smaller gang—the Bishops—allied themselves to the Chaplains.

Our Jefferson Avenue neighborhood sported the El Quintos and their allies—the Tiny Tims and the Stompers. All were united against the hated Chaplains. Each of these groups claimed hundreds of members, but that probably was a gross exaggeration. Yet each gang did contain a hard-core leadership of ten to fifteen clearly sociopathic youth willing to do anything to increase the power and prestige of their gang. In 1954 this period of increasing crime and gang warfare occurred just as my family moved from 709 Halsey Street to 84 Ralph Avenue, three blocks away. Halsey had quickly deteriorated into a classic slum street, far too menacing for my widowed mom and two younger sisters. None of the O'Kanes regretted leaving Halsey Street with its simmering potential for violence.

Our new Ralph Avenue apartment occupied the top floor of a three-story building, the ground floor of which housed an ice cream parlor that clearly had seen better days. Across the street, a group of gypsies illegally occupied an abandoned store. My sisters, to the consternation of our mom, would regularly enter the gypsy abode to play with the young girls there. Nothing ever happened to them though I worried they'd eventually be cut up and cannibalized. True to gypsy custom, when the landlord of that store finally demanded his rent, they packed up and disappeared. They never even said goodbye to Helen and Bunny, both of whom had been captivated by the gypsies' dresses and jewelry and by their storefront, which was covered with vividly colored satin drapes.

Around us, urban blight became an increasingly common feature of the neighborhood with abandoned stores, vandalized buildings, and burned out apartments more and more apparent. The area was rapidly skidding into true slum status, and Mammy's fear and anxiety mounted daily. In the light of this rapidly deteriorating situation, all my friends increasingly "hung out" at Our Lady of Good Counsel as a way to avoid the "dangerous classes" now roaming the neighborhood.

The summers of 1955 and 1956 witnessed the growing violence between the El Quintos and the Chaplains, along with their allies. In those summer months, a street murder a week was not uncommon and gave rise to what the New York press termed the "long hot summer," referring not to the climate, but to the upsurge in gang violence.

In Brooklyn, gang wars never occurred in large-scale encounters, and gang fights between El Quintos and Chaplains clearly remained impossible even if their gang leaders desired an all-out battle. The explicit reason for a war masked the real intent for violence — to gain status or rep within the neighborhood. The more violent the gang, the better, since violence and status worked together in reinforcing each other. Violence meant prestige.

The attempt to organize a gang war in our area clearly involved a surrealistic, bizarre system in its scheduling and rules of combat, arranged at a gang parlay not unlike a major mafia sit down. While mafiosi attempted to first resolve their respective differences, the war counselors of rival Brooklyn street gangs simply arranged the violence straightaway. The when, what, and where of a proposed gang fight was duly sealed in an "agreement" with handshakes, chest thumping, and, in our neighborhood, a milk shake or ice cream soda at the neutral ground of Meyer's Ice Cream Parlor on Broadway. The gang leaders had possibly seen too many medieval knight movies depicting the chivalrous codes of old, so they played at mimicking the noble knights' codes of behavior as presented in the many films of the 1950s, including *Ivanhoe, The Black Shield of Falworth, Knights of the Round Table,* and *Tales of Robin Hood.* In their romanticized world, the gang warriors thought they were emulating the noble deeds seen on the silver screen. These ideals, however, never really materialized, and the gang's exploits more clearly evoked Monte Python's *Holy Grail* antics than any code of chivalry.

I clearly recall one war parlay between the El Quintos and the Chaplains. Napoleon, the war counselor of the El Quintos, and his three Irish lieutenants (the Molloy brothers — Acey, Deucey, and Blackie) sat down with their Chaplain counterparts to arrange the impending gang war. Everything short of a duly notarized written declaration of war resulted. The only thing missing was a gauntlet to throw down on the floor of the ice cream parlor. With the time and conditions of the impending gang war agreed upon, the protagonists finished their sodas and returned to their gangs to organize the fight.

Yet when the night of the authorized gang war arrived, no fight ensued. Predictably, everyone in the neighborhood knew about the proposed fight since all of the sociopathic El Quintos bragged about it, and sure enough, one of the Jefferson Avenue mothers alerted police at the 81st Precinct. When the night of the battle arrived, practically the entire neighborhood appeared to witness the anticipated carnage (from a safe distance, of course). Members of the El Quintos, Stompers, and Tiny Tims mulled around the BMT's Gates Avenue station of the El as they awaited the arrival of the Chaplains and Bishops, traveling economy style on the subway. As the invaders descended the El's platform stairs, rocks, pieces of lumber, and beer bottles, all thrown by the enemy below, rained upon them. They halted their descent and quickly retreated back to the platform, boarding the next train away from the battlefield. The police arrived and, with their billy clubs, quickly dispersed the remaining El Quinto warriors. So ended the so-called gang war, an ignominious humbling defeat for the Chaplains.

Other gang "wars" ended in a similar fashion. Since the gang members often bragged about upcoming battles, police knew about them through the neighborhood grapevine and broke up any fight with their fists and nightsticks before any actual battle could begin. I recall one such encounter later that summer as I looked out my Ralph Avenue window late one Saturday night. Some twenty El Quintos had assembled a block away. Suddenly a number of 81st Precinct squad cars, loaded with rookie cops dressed in their telltale blue/gray uniforms, arrived and attacked the group. With clubs flailing and gangsters fleeing, there was no quarter given and no questions asked. These rookie cop "orientation sessions" prepared police for life on Bedford-Stuyvesant streets.

Even though large-scale gang wars rarely occurred, individual gang killings regularly took place. After the El Quinto-Chaplain gang encounter failed to materialize, the humiliated Chaplains sought their revenge, seeking to restore their lost honor after having fled the field of battle. This revenge usually took the form of "japing" wherein three or four Chaplains or Bishops would enter El Quinto or Tiny Tim or Stomper territory and murder any gangster whom they encountered, a lone victim isolated from his gang. A week later, three or four El Quintos would do the same to a Chaplain victim, thus restoring the larger gang's honor and rep. Nothing went unavenged. And anyone could easily become an innocent victim of violent gang behavior if he were a wrong person in the wrong place.

Another writer, David Van Pelt, sent me a June 18, 1955 *New York Times* clipping detailing one such murder that I'd forgotten, though it certainly had mesmerized the neighborhood. Three Chaplains murdered a sixteen-year-old leader of the Tiny Tims in retaliation for the earlier shotgun killing of a fifteen-year-old Chaplain. Poised on the roof of a five-story tenement, the Chaplain aimed and shot his .32 caliber rifle at his Tiny Tim victim, killing him instantly. Police later arrested him and his sixteen-year-old accomplices.

Such cyclical violence and retribution characterized the summer months of the late 1950s. For the gangs, no insult could go unanswered. Harlem, East Harlem, Williamsburg, South Brooklyn, and the Bronx witnessed similar violence from 1955 through 1959. Mass hysteria also afflicted entire neighborhoods with rumors of impending violence.

I recall another incident where a rumor spread throughout most of Brooklyn's high schools that a Bronx gang — the Fordham Baldies — were about to descend on Brooklyn, killing any teens they encountered. If my memory stands correct, this would have been in the late spring of 1957. So widespread was the intense fear that Bishop Loughlin and Brooklyn Prep actually canceled classes. As luck would have it, my high school, Cathedral Prep Seminary, ignored the hysteria and my classmates and I had to forgo a free day, probably risking being murdered by a wild Baldie because our school's prefect of discipline put no substance in the gang's threat. But Fordham Baldies never attacked Brooklyn. They probably didn't know how to get there from the Bronx.

Throughout these long, hot summers, police regularly stopped my group and often frisked us, searching for hidden weapons like knives or brass knuckles. None were found except for one teen's small pen knife, which the cops confiscated.

The most interesting gang leader of all — at least to me since I knew him before he was to become the war counselor of the El Quintos — was none other than Napoleon. Let me point out that I looked more like the historical Napoleon than he did. Both of us attended Our Lady of Good Counsel elementary school and served as altar boys in the parish church. Quiet yet friendly, Napoleon often played with me on Halsey Street where we both lived. This was an unusual friendship since he was black and I was Irish. Big and strong at six feet two inches and two hundred pounds, Napoleon even commanded respect at age twelve, and I could always count on him if I needed help. As it turned out one day, my eighth-grade class at Our Lady of Good Counsel needed his help. In the spring of 1954 word quickly spread around our school that the P.S. 26 kids planned to attack and "destroy" us. Our teachers, tough Brooklyn Franciscan Brothers, heard the rumor and quickly devised an ambush where we would "get them before they got us." Of course Napoleon played a key role in this scenario. When the P.S. 26 kids arrived, they had to enter a narrow passageway leading to our inner school yard where they were jumped by Napoleon and Brothers Owen, Ralph, Lawrence, Robert, Alan, and Demas, as well as the rest of the eighth-graders. Kicking, punching, "head hunting," and biting were the battle plans and the invaders fled in panic. All agreed Napoleon and his white lieutenants, the Molloy brothers, as well as Brother Owen and Brother Lawrence had distinguished themselves in the front line of that battle. I cheered them on from the back of the maelstrom since I told myself I shouldn't risk hurting one of the P.S. 26 raiders even more.

After we graduated from Our Lady of Good Counsel, things changed for most of us, but particularly for Napoleon. He attended Boys High School where he joined the El Quintos and received his new gang name, Napoleon, and rose to become the gang's war counselor, the most important position of any gang of that era. He quickly distinguished himself through his use of violence and became feared and respected by everyone. His exploits, however, doomed him. On one occasion he kicked a rival Chaplain to death but somehow beat the rap. A year later he murdered another Chaplain with a machete. The last I knew, he'd been committed to a prison hospital for the criminally insane.

By 1956, race had become a dominant feature of the neighborhood's violence. My friends and I, all white, feared walking in certain streets where we would be attacked by black teens. Earlier in the decade, the El Quintos had integrated. Napoleon's three body guards, the Molloy brothers, were Irish, and the gang, while overwhelmingly black, also boasted white Irish, Puerto Rican, and Italian members. These multi-ethnic El Quintos would literally strut around the neighborhood, with Napoleon leading them. All were arrayed in black leather outfits, carrying broom handles and garrison belts as well as concealed knives and zip guns, which were homemade revolvers that fired a single .22

caliber bullet. Often they were so inaccurate that they misfired, injuring and sometimes killing the shooter. One Irish Stomper even had a black umbrella with a spring-loaded stiletto at its tip which he delighted showing to all around him.

Acey, Deucey and Blackie, Napoleon's three bodyguards, were misfits: two clearly could be considered sociopathic while the third was only dim-witted. One night the latter, Acey, accompanied by a black fellow gangster, broke into a sporting goods store on Broadway. When the burglar alarm sounded, the black teen took off while the Irish kid hid under the store's counter for a full forty-five minutes at which time the police finally arrived. Arrested, Acey quickly gave up his fellow burglar and both were transported to the 81st Precinct where the Irish thief was handed over to an Irish detective and the black thief to a black detective. Each detective severely beat the teen in his charge. A day later, we saw Acey clearly had been worked over—a standard practice in those days. We asked him why he hid in the store rather than escaping, and he responded, "I was scared and didn't know what to do, so I hid under the counter."

By the late 1950s, race trumped everything else and the gangs split completely along racial and ethnic membership. The El Quintos and Chaplains became all-black gangs while the Stompers were all white, even though its membership quickly dwindled with the exodus of whites from the neighbor-hood.

In spite of this, I still have a fondness for Napo-leon. My friendship with him did pay off on one memorable occasion. One afternoon, a group of six or seven of my friends and I lounged on a stoop on Putnam Avenue when a group of fifteen to twenty El Quintos, led by Napoleon, appeared from around the corner. Normally that meant that we would have been attacked and beaten, but Napo-leon halted any violence as he glanced at me, nod-ded in silent recognition, and led his group away.

On another occasion, Napoleon's absence from his group almost did us in. One night seven of our group had just left Meyer's Ice Cream Parlor on Broadway. As we walked on Howard Avenue, we could see, a block away, approximately two dozen El Quintos. As soon as they spotted us, they decid-ed to attack and chased us. But we had a city block's head start. I ran to my apartment on Ralph Avenue, and the rest ran to the Our Lady of Good Counsel rectory where Father McCabe sheltered them. The El Quintos paused at the corner of Ralph and Putnam avenues in front of the Philbin's gro-cery store, where they encountered a police officer on foot patrol. Even from my third-floor window I could see the terror on the young cop's face as he was surrounded by more than fifteen El Quintos. He grabbed one of them and wrote down his name and address. The rest ran around him in pursuit of my friends, who made it safely to the rectory. An hour later, Father McCabe called our downstairs neighbor to find out what had happened to me. All had assumed I'd been caught, beaten, and possibly killed since I hadn't joined them in the race to the rectory. Father McCabe then drove each of our group to his respective home. All's well that ends well, I suppose, but that was close.

The continuing anxiety over gang violence and personal safety permeated our daily existence. A simple walk down a street became a conundrum: *Should I walk down this particular street? Or should I avoid it lest I be jumped by the El Quintos? What particular gang kids live on that street?* As my sisters recently reminded me, each day we worried about being attacked and beaten by someone.

As a result of such mental calculations, my group rarely took the shortest route between two places. Instead, we'd look down a street first to see if any gangsters were there. If so, we walked one or two streets around the "obstacle," avoiding an attack. The rule of thumb dictated that streets with lots of pedestrian traffic were safe. On empty streets gang members might quickly emerge from their citadels to attack. Even today I avoid empty streets in New York City where possible, even though crime statistics indicate that such streets actually are quite safe. Even where I live in affluent, safe Madison, I often lock my front door as I bring out the garbage since I never know who might break in and jump me. Paranoia lingers.

The art of walking in a high-crime area entails what has been called "street smarts," a mental construct that enables people to navigate through potentially violent encounters. Street smarts alert one to problematic situations and provide "codes" of behavior: Never stare at another teenager. Never walk down empty streets. If possible, run from unexpected hostile groups rather than confront them. Never display outright fear when crossing paths with potential troublemakers. Carry yourself as if you have a weapon, even if you do not. If confronted, do something completely unexpected to confuse or befuddle the other guy.

In spite of these codes, I had to learn the hard way. One afternoon, as I waited for a bus on Broadway, a skinny, puny El Quinto appeared out of nowhere; he weighed even less than I did. As he stared at me, I stared back at him—a game of upmanship. If I didn't stare him down, it would alert him that I feared him. He approached me and asked what I was looking at, to which I replied, "You!" Next thing I remember was a fist blow to my left temple. I never saw it coming! He then marched off. That's the last time I tried to stare down anyone. I'm happy he didn't pull a knife on me or shoot me for so obviously "disrespecting" him.

One of our group, Moose, epitomized urban smarts in a particularly graphic manner. In late summer in 1956, on a very humid, 95-degree Sunday afternoon, word went out that Pat Walsh's family would be visiting relatives, which meant that his apartment would be available for a beer party. Pat duly informed us of this bonanza and all agreed that our group would assemble at 1 p.m. on the corner of Jefferson and Howard avenues in front of Katz's luncheonette. Our group that afternoon comprised Johnny McClorey, Peter Fiorillo, Pat Connelly, Kenny McNally, Danny Feldman, Richie Heraty, Louie Mione, Mike Rockwood, and me. We had our six-packs of beer and a few bottles of Gallo Muscatel and Port, our premier wines, all in brown paper bags and purchased a day earlier at the local store whose owner never questioned or carded us even though we were all only fifteen years old.

At 1 p.m. Moose also joined the group. Though he had never previously been a close member of our pack, he heard about the rendezvous and simply appeared. A big fellow, Moose scaled two hundred pounds and stood about six feet three inches tall. Never very athletic, average in his school work, and nondescript in his appearance, he didn't command the respect or admiration of any in the group. Since he was there, though, we let him join us.

There was, however, one major problem. Pat Walsh lived one block away on Jefferson Avenue between Howard and Saratoga avenues, a block infested with El Quintos. Curiously, that street had been designated a Play Street by the city, but none of us went there since it remained too dangerous. Since Pat Walsh lived on the street, on the gang's turf, he was viewed by El Quintos as safe. But we had no such claim to protection if confronted by them. Thus a decision had to be made: should we walk down Jefferson to Pat's house, risking attack, or should we walk to Putnam, go down Putnam, circle back on Saratoga, and enter Jefferson from that direction since that route avoided the El Quintos? Our leader Johnny McClorey decided we should not tempt fate and should take the longer route. But Moose announced that he would go straight there. Never known for his agility or swiftness, he didn't want to exert himself beyond what was necessary. After all, it was 95 degrees and he didn't want to take the longer route. He asked, "What chance is there that we'll be jumped?" We couldn't believe it and figured he was crazy. So the rest of the group ran down Howard to Putnam, made a right on Putnam, right on Saratoga, and right on Jefferson, raced up three flights of stairs to Pat's apartment, and went straight to the front windows to observe Moose's possible demise. Clearly we anticipated what might happen and that we might be eyewitnesses to The End Of Moose.

Heavy and slow, Moose plodded down Jefferson with not a soul in sight. Suddenly at mid-block, five El Quintos emerged from a tenement. Blind drunk, they threw beer bottles across the street at an elderly woman walking by. Fortunately, they missed their target. Moose had not yet been spotted. Seeing the gangsters, he froze in his tracks. He faced limited choices: He could turn around and run back to Howard Avenue and duck into Katz's, but he would easily be caught since he ran so slowly. He could cross the street and walk beyond the El Quintos, but urban smarts told him that would be disastrous since it clearly signaled that he was a coward. He could stay his course and walk past the gangsters but undoubtedly would be attacked since he was a stranger to them and on their turf. Or he could duck into a building's hallway and wait till the coast cleared, hoping he wouldn't be spotted. (I actually did this months earlier in a similar situation as I attempted to visit Walsh. I spotted several El Quintos and ended up hiding in a hallway for three hours. Residents of the building asked me what I was doing there as they entered or exited, and I smiled and said, "Oh, I'm just resting here. It's so hot outside.")

We watched and waited for Moose to decide. He opted for an ingenious and truly memorable gambit. He walked right up to the El Quintos, dragging one leg, his body bent completely over, drooling, with his tongue hanging out, spastically shaking, and stammered at them in almost unintelligible, slurred English, while he asked for help in locating Walsh's apartment house. Brilliant! The drunken El Quintos actually walked him there! Three stories up, we gazed at the scene, completely impressed. When he arrived, we asked Moose why he did what he did. He responded that he was scared so he felt he would do something truly bizarre so the El Quintos would pity him. He said, "I wanted them to feel sorry for me."

For the next three hours we played poker and consumed our beer and wine, tidied Walsh's apartment so his parents would never know what occurred, and debated on our exit. As we looked out the window, we noticed that the gangsters were still there—more drunk than before. We decided to depart along the same long route by which we had arrived. But again Moose decided differently, announcing that he would go in the same spastic, crippled, slurring manner in which he'd come. And so he did. The rest of us raced to Katz's luncheonette and waited there, watching Moose shamble past the El Quintos who, incredibly, greeted him and wished him well. At a safe distance, he finally shed his disguise and with the rest of us ran from Walsh's street.

Moose gained our group's esteem for his truly innovative manner in avoiding harm. Henceforth he was invited to all our groups' parties, basketball games, and treks. Years later, crossing Flatbush with my six-year-old son J.B., I suddenly encountered Moose. He yelled to me from a cab that he drove and told me he'd become a cop with the New York Police Department and drove a taxi for extra income. In the middle of traffic with irate drivers cursing at us, we both reminisced about his El Quinto encounter and had a great laugh about it.

The old neighborhood had become quite dangerous. Its rapid decline into criminality was reflected in the defensive actions of other residents of the area as well. The Bushwick Avenue office of Dr. Bodkin, our friendly neighborhood physician, had turned into an armed fortress. In 1956 I arrived there for a checkup and noticed that his front reception room sported two large Doberman Pinschers, both poised to devour anyone who might incur the Doc's wrath. Later as I sat at his desk and chatted, I spotted a loaded shotgun next to him. Curious, I asked, "Why the weapon?" He said, "It's there so I can blow the head off any #$@!* druggie or robber who tries to attack me!" Fierce dogs, loaded shotgun, and a man quite willing and able to unleash these "deterrents" attest to the descent of the old neighborhood into darkness and fear.

Violent gangs, fears for one's personal safety, and an increasingly blighted neighborhood all coalesced to encourage moves to better areas. By 1959 all of our gang had moved out. Most of us moved to either the Bushwick section of Brooklyn or the neighboring areas of Queens, such as Richmond

Hill, Ridgewood, and Woodhaven. Decades later, most of our group had settled in Staten Island, Long Island, and the outer sections of Queens. Johnny McClorey settled in Australia and Victor Herbert resided in Phoenix, Arizona before returning to Queens. At a reunion, we all roared with laughter at the great times and escapades we'd had. Each of us remarked how grateful he was for the parish of Our Lady of Good Counsel, the Franciscan Brothers and parish priests, the Knights of Columbus, and the Holy Name Society men who tried to help us and serve as role models. Rough and tumble as some of them were, they somehow guided us, steering us from delinquent careers and violent gang membership. Alas! Our Lady of Good Counsel is almost gone, merged with the neighboring parish of St. John the Baptist. Its golden age of the 1940s and 1950s is nothing but a fond memory for those of us who lived in that colorful, vibrant time.

Epilogue

A new era and a new life unfolded for me in 1958. A college education at St. Francis, graduate study at Columbia University and New York University, and summer volunteer work in Puerto Rico, Mexico, and Peru broadened my horizons immensely. I held various overlapping part-time jobs, some lasting only for holiday seasons and summers: grave "landscaper" at St. John's cemetery in Queens; messenger for Parker Brothers Insurance in New York; worker in the U.S. Postal Service; liquor delivery man for Wall Street firms; messenger for Manufacturer's Trust Company; filing clerk for Health Insurance Plan in Brooklyn;

and usher at the Brooklyn Academy of Music. Finally, I landed a full-time teaching job in 1964 at my alma mater, St. Francis College. There I taught sociology for three years and met and married my wife Marge, a nurse who headed Student Health Services. How I came to date one of the few females in an all-male college is another story! We married in 1966 and, a year later, came to Madison, New Jersey, where I taught sociology at Drew University for thirty nine years and where the family grew up. Retiring in 2006 has given me plenty of time to reminisce.

I now realize how much my early years in Bedford-Stuyvesant have influenced my sociological career and how the encounters with the neighborhood gangs lured me into criminology as a specialization. The murder of Otto the shoemaker, the friendship with Napoleon, the plight of living in a blighted apartment building with greedy landlords, the "watching over my shoulder" to avoid victimization—all of these led to my fascination with the urban world and all its ethnic groups and ever-changing neighborhoods as well as the sad cycle of violence and murder so endemic in lower-income areas. Credit is also due to Mammy and Grandma Tilda who likewise were mesmerized by the violence both in Northern Ireland and New York. I still recall lying awake on Sunday nights as they discussed the latest murders chronicled every

Collection of James M. O'Kane

On our wedding day (1966).

week in the Sunday edition of New York's *Daily News*.

Jefferson Avenue, with its characters and situations, represents a small snapshot of Brooklyn life sixty years ago, an era never to be repeated, frozen as if in a time capsule. It was our era and we loved it.

Acknowledgments

Writing this book has brought back so many long-lost memories of life on Jefferson Avenue and its surrounding neighborhood. But my memories alone could not account accurately for all that I have transcribed. Others helped enormously in these recollections, most notably my sister Helen Grubbs whose phenomenal recall corrected and sharpened many of the anecdotes contained in this volume. Also, my sister Bernadette (Bunny) Moran reminded me of much of the information about our mother and grandmother. Credit here also is due to her daughter, my niece Margaret Mary, whose English class essay about the life of my mother, written almost twenty years ago, helped flesh out her story. I also thank my Uncle Dan for his aid in filling in the gaps in the family's saga in Northern Ireland.

I owe enormous credit to my buddies from childhood. Some of us reconnected after a lapse of almost fifty years. When I decided to write this tome I sought them out, and we had a number of reunions at which we had a grand time reminiscing about the escapades of our childhood. Foremost among these friends are: Johnny McClorey, now residing in Australia, who closely edited virtually every sentence in the book and in so doing kept me howling with laughter; Peter Fiorillo, whose memory startles me as he recounted life on the street, particularly about what it was like being an Italian among Irish friends; Pat Walsh, whose realistic accounts of the area gangs reminded me of the dangers of the street; Victor Herbert, my high school classmate, who filled in many of the gaps on our elementary school days, often in hilarious fashion; Pat Connelly and his wife Rosie, who in many ways became the heart and soul of our group and who vividly reminded me of the exciting times we had as teens, particularly in the social events in our parish church; and Richie Heraty, who reminded all of us how dangerous and chaotic our teenage years had been. Without these buddies, this book would never have been completed.

Acknowledgments

Special thanks also is extended to those friends and colleagues in the Madison area who read and critiqued parts of the book. Here I would single out Dr. Jim Mills and Dr. Phil Jensen (Drew University), Dr. John Coverdale (Seton Hall Law School), Fred Luhmann, and Nick Finamore, who offered friendly advice on parts of the work; David Van Pelt, who is writing a book on Brooklyn gangs and gave me needed information of the gangs of that era; and Gamin Bartle and her staff at Drew's faculty Lab who helped with the maps. I also thank Dean Bill Rogers (Drew University) and graduate student Jaclyn Harte, who provided both encouragement and the actual production of this memoir. Without them, particularly Jaclyn, this book could not have been produced.

A nod goes out to the *Madison Eagle*, my hometown paper, which published an earlier version of the chapter about my adventures at the Monroe theater in 1980.

Grateful thanks are extended to Pat Carr, who did a superb job editing the book, and Lorraine and Bill Ash, the publishers of Cape House Books. Lorraine, a former Drew student of mine, has been a faithful friend over the past twenty-five years. Her encouragement, exuberant personality, and excellent editing and organizing abilities provided me with the push I needed to complete this project.

Finally I must thank my wife Marge for all the encouragement and insights she provided, spurring me on to put my anecdotal accounts onto paper. Her calmness and ability to zero in on the heart of these stories aided me immensely. Thanks also to my sons James (J.B.), Dan, Pat, Joe and my daughter Mary Rose, who suffered all those years listening to my rants and raves about the old days.

About the Author

J ames M. O'Kane, Professor Emeritus of Sociology, taught at Drew University in Madison, New Jersey from 1967 until retiring in 2006. He received his Ph.D. in Educational Sociology from New York University, his M.S. in Social Work from Columbia University, and his B.A. degree in Economics from St. Francis College in Brooklyn, New York. He has authored more than

Collection of James M. O'Kane

James O'Kane circa 1951.

fifty articles as well as three books: *Pamplona: A Sociological Analysis of Migration and Urban Adaptation Patterns* (1981); *The Crooked Ladder: Gangsters, Ethnicity, and the American Dream* (1992) and *Wicked Deeds: Murder in America* (2005). He has been quoted in newspapers including *The New York Times, The Christian Science Monitor, USA Today, The Boston Globe, The Baltimore Sun, The Philadelphia Inquirer, Houston Chronicle,* and *The Miami Herald.* He also has been featured in an in-depth interview on the *MacNeil/Lehrer NewsHour* on the topic of homicide. He currently lives in Madison, New Jersey, with his wife Margaret.

Collection of James M. O'Kane

James O'Kane today.

Visit James M. O'Kane at www.Jim-OKane.com.

Appendix

Ancestors of James O'Kane

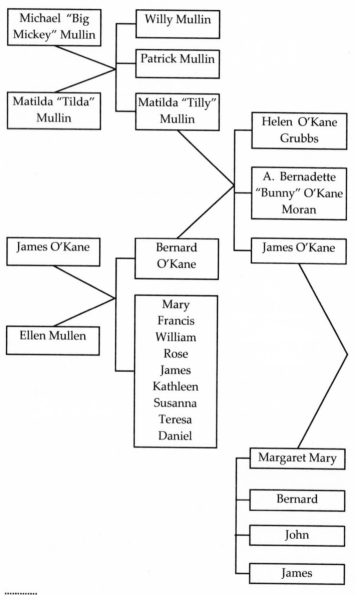

Descendants of James O'Kane

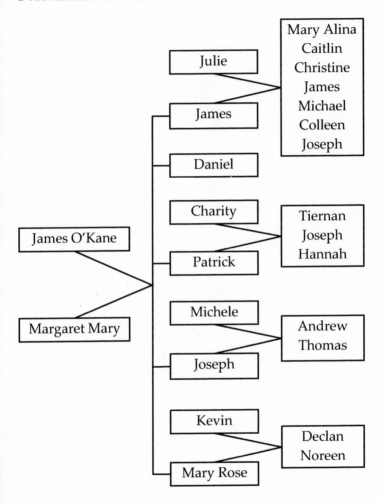

Map of New York showing Bedford-Stuyvesant

Based on a public domain map on Wikipedia, www.Wikipedia.org

The five boroughs of New York, showing the Bedford-Stuyvesant neighborhood of Brooklyn.

Neighborhood map

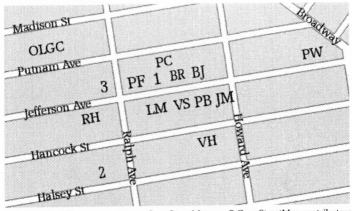

Based on a map at www.OpenStreetMap.org © OpenStreetMap contributors

My childhood neighborhood, showing homes and highlights.

1 – *My first house, 899 Jefferson Avenue*
2 – *My second house, 709 Halsey Street*
3 – *My third house, 84 Ralph Avenue*
BJ – *Bop Jones*
BR – *Billy Ritchie*
JM – *Johnny McClorey*
LM – *Louie Minoe / Joey Mazolla*
OLGC – *Our Lady of Good Counsel*
PB – *Paddy Barrigan*
PC – *Pat Connelly*
PF – *Peter Fiorillo*
PW – *Pat Walsh*
RH – *Richie Heraty*
VH – *Victor Herbert*
VS – *Vinny Sinerchia*